Indochina Monographs

RLG Military Operations and Activities in the Laotian Panhandle

by

Brig. Gen. Soutchay Vongsavanh

U.S. ARMY CENTER OF MILITARY HISTORY
WASHINGTON, D.C.

Library of Congress Cataloging in Publication Data

Vongsavanh, Soutchay.
　　RLG military operations and activities in the Laotian panhandle.

　　(Indochina monograph)
　　1. Vietnamese Conflict, 1961-1975--Campaigns--Laos.
2. Laos--History. I. Title. II. Title: R.L.G. military
operations and activities in the Laotian panhandle.
III. Series.
DS557.8.L3V66　　　959.704'34　　　81-10934
　　　　　　　　　　　　　　　　　AACR2

Reprinted 1984

CMH PUB 92-19

This book is not copyrighted and may be reproduced in
whole or in part without consulting the publisher

Indochina Monographs

This is one of a series originally published in limited quantity in 1980 by the U.S. Army Center of Military History. The continuous demand for these monographs has prompted reprinting. They were written by officers who held responsible positions in the Cambodian, Laotian, and South Vietnamese armed forces during the war in Indochina. The General Research Corporation provided writing facilities and other necessary support under an Army contract with the Center of Military History. The monographs were not edited or altered and reflect the views of their authors--not necessarily those of the U.S. Army or the Department of Defense. The authors were not attempting to write definitive accounts but to set down how they saw the war in Southeast Asia.

These works should provide useful source materials for serious historians pending publication of the more definitive series, the <u>U.S. Army in Vietnam</u>.

                                            DOUGLAS KINNARD
                                      Brigadier General, USA (Ret)
                                      Chief of Military History

INDOCHINA MONOGRAPHS

TITLES IN THE SERIES
(title--author/s--LC Catalog Card)

The Cambodian Incursion--Brig. Gen. Tran Dinh Tho--79-21722 — CMH PUB 92-4

The Easter Offensive of 1972--Lt. Gen. Ngo Quang Truong--79-20551 — CMH PUB 92-13

The General Offensives of 1968-69--Col. Hoang Ngoc Lung--80-607931 — CMH PUB 92-6

Intelligence--Col. Hoang Ngoc Lung--81-10844/AACR2 — CMH PUB 92-14

The Khmer Republic at War and the Final Collapse--Lt. Gen. Sak Sutsakhan--79-607776 — CMH PUB 92-5

Lam Son 719--Maj. Gen. Nguyen Duy Hinh--79-607101 — CMH PUB 92-2

Leadership--General Cao Van Vien--80-607941 — CMH PUB 92-12

Pacification--Brig. Gen. Tran Dinh Tho--79-607913 — CMH PUB 92-11

RLG Military Operations and Activities in the Laotian Panhandle--Brig. Gen. Soutchay Vongsavanh--81-10934/AACR2 — CMH PUB 92-19

The RVNAF--Lt. Gen. Dong Van Khuyen--79-607963 — CMH PUB 92-7

RVNAF and U.S. Operational Cooperation and Coordination--Lt. Gen. Ngo Quang Truong--79-607170 — CMH PUB 92-16

RVNAF Logistics--Lt. Gen. Dong Van Khuyen--80-607117 — CMH PUB 92-17

Reflections on the Vietnam War--General Cao Van Vien and Lt. Gen. Dong Van Khuyen--79-607979 — CMH PUB 92-8

The Royal Lao Army and U.S. Army Advice and Support--Maj. Gen. Oudone Sananikone--79-607054 — CMH PUB 92-10

The South Vietnamese Society--Maj. Gen. Nguyen Duy Hinh and Brig. Gen. Tran Dinh Tho--79-17694 — CMH PUB 92-18

Strategy and Tactics--Col. Hoang Ngoc Lung--79-607102 — CMH PUB 92-15

Territorial Forces--Lt. Gen. Ngo Quang Truong--80-15131 — CMH PUB 92-9

The U.S. Adviser--General Cao Van Vien, Lt. Gen. Ngo Quang Truong, Lt. Gen. Dong Van Khuyen, Maj. Gen. Nguyen Duy Hinh, Brig. Gen. Tran Dinh Tho, Col. Hoang Ngoc Lung, and Lt. Col. Chu Xuan Vien--80-607108 — CMH PUB 92-1

Vietnamization and the Cease-Fire--Maj. Gen. Nguyen Duy Hinh--79-607982 — CMH PUB 92-3

The Final Collapse--General Cao Van Vien--81-607989 — CMH PUB 90-26

Preface

The Kingdom of Laos, because of geographical location, was destined to play a major role as North Vietnam endeavored to expand her area of influence throughout Indochina. This is especially true of the Laotian Panhandle which borders both South Vietnam and Cambodia. Following the March 1970 coup in Cambodia, the closure of the port of Sihanoukville to the Communists and the increasing effectiveness of navy Market Time barrier operations, southern Laos became even more important to the enemy for the movement of supplies and men to support Communist activities in South Vietnam and Cambodia.

This monograph reviews and analyzes Royal Lao Government military operations and activities in the Laotian Panhandle. I have devoted special attention to the significance of the panhandle for enemy military operations in South Vietnam and Cambodia, the initiation of conventional warfare in southern Laos, lessons learned during the employment of regular and irregular forces and developments following the 1973 cease-fire. As author, I am fortunate to be able to draw on my personal experience as Commanding General of Military Region 4 from 1 July 1971 until my exodus 13 June 1975.

I am indebted to General Oudone Sananikone, former Chief of Staff for the Royal Lao Armed Forces and subsequently Under Secretary, Ministry of National Defense, for his guidance, assistance and comprehensive knowledge of developments in Laos. I am especially grateful for his review and critique of my final draft with the objective of providing a highly professional contribution to the Indochina Refugee-Authored Monograph Program.

Finally, I wish to express my personal appreciation to Ms. Pham Thi Bong. Ms. Bong, a former Captain in the Republic of Vietnam Armed Forces, devoted long hours typing, editing and in the administrative preparation of my manuscript in final form.

                                                Soutchay Vongsavanh
                                                Brigadier General, RLA

McLean, Virginia
21 February 1978

Contents

Chapter	Page
I. INTRODUCTION	1
The Laos Panhandle	1
The Ho Chi Minh Trail	4
The Sihanouk Trail	14
The Pathet Lao	17
Relations Between the Pathet Lao and the NVA	18
Significant Developments Following the 1962 Geneva Agreement	20
II. THE ORGANIZATION AND EMPLOYMENT OF IRREGULAR FORCES IN SOUTHERN LAOS	23
The Military Regions	23
Interdiction of the NVA Logistics System in the Panhandle	25
South Vietnamese Activities in the Panhandle	29
Coordination between Cambodia and Laos in the Panhandle	31
Laos Irregulars Before 1970	33
Laos Irregulars After 1970	41
Command Problems	44
III. THE INITIATION OF CONVENTIONAL WARFARE IN SOUTHERN LAOS	51
Attopeu	54
Saravane	56
Tchepone	58
IV. THE NVA PANHANDLE OFFENSIVES OF 1971 AND 1972	63
Paksong and Route 23	65
Reorganization	70
Saravane	72
Khong Sedone	79
Saravane Again and the Approach of Cease-Fire	81
V. DEVELOPMENTS FOLLOWING THE FEBRUARY 1973 CEASE-FIRE	87
Agreement to Restore Peace and Achieve National Concord	87
Violations of the Cease-Fire	95
Reduction of Royal Lao Military Strength	97

Chapter	Page
VI. OBSERVATIONS AND CONCLUSIONS	102
Successes and Failures	102
Observations	106

Appendix

A. THE AGREEMENT ON THE RESTORATION OF PEACE AND RECONCILIATION IN LAOS. 111
   General Principles 111
   Military Provisions 112
   Provisions on Political Affairs 113
   The Joint Commission for Implementation of the Agreement and the International Commission for Supervision and Control 115

B. PROTOCOLS TO THE AGREEMENT. 117
   Summary of Main Provisions 117

GLOSSARY 119

Charts

No.		Page
1.	The Irregular Organization in Military Region IV Before 1970	36
2.	Lao Irregular Heavy Weapons Company (Organic to GM)	42
3.	Lao Irregular Battalion (Organic to GM)	43
4.	The Organization Irregular Forces in MR IV After 1970	45
5.	Organization of Irregular Forces in Military Region III After 1970	46
6.	Organization of Military Region IV in September 1971	73

Maps

No.		Page
1.	The Key Position of Laos in Indochina	2
2.	Ho Chi Minh Trail	6
3.	Annual Rainfall in Laos	7
4.	The Ho Chi Minh Trail After 1970	8
5.	The Enemy Base Area Complex in Eastern MR III and MR IV	10
6.	Sihanouk Trail	15
7.	Indochina Military Regions	24
8.	Zones of Control and the Ho Chi Minh Trail	26
9.	The Guerrilla Zones in Military Region IV Before 1970	39
10.	The Battle of Attopeu	55
11.	The Battle of Paksong	69
12.	The Battle of Saravane	75
13.	The Battle of Khong Sedone	82

Illustrations

	Page
Heavily Camouflaged NVA Storage Bunker on the Ho Chi Minh Trail near Tchepone in the Laos Panhandle	11
North Vietnamese Petroleum Pipe Line in the Laos Panhandle. The installation was under air attack at the time this photo was taken (probably in 1972).	13
Camouflaged storage bunker on the Ho Chi Minh Trail in the Laos Panhandle. A road-widening bulldozer has cut into the bank revealing the hidden entrance and destroying a bicycle	28
A South Vietnamese Army Unit advances in the Laos panhandle near Tchepone in Operation Lam Son 719, February 1971	32
Laos Irregulars in Training at an Irregular Base Camp on the Plateau des Bolovens Before 1970	34
In Lam Son 719, South Vietnamese soldiers ran a captured NVA amphibious tank. This Soviet-built light tank mounted a 76-mm gun	59
Troops of BV 44 Assemble in the Saravane Area	66
NVA Ammunition Truck Destroyed by Air Attack in Support of the Saravane Operation	76
Pathet Lao at Wattay Airport Waiting to Unload Another Soviet Transport	94
Soviet Transports Used to Bring the Pathet Lao into Vientiane at Wattay Airport	94

CHAPTER I

Introduction

In the years following World War II and the demise of the French colonial empire in Indochina, Laos bore a tragic resemblance to the small state of Belgium, which like Laos, was an unwilling but helpless battleground of its larger, more powerful neighbors. No external power coveted Laos for its wealth — it was surely the most undeveloped, poorest state in the region — or actively sought its support in a larger alliance. But it occupied, by the arbitrary politics of its boundaries and its geographical situation, a position that impelled the North Vietnamese to occupy and use its territory in the furtherance of the conquest of South Vietnam. *(Map 1)* The part of Laos essential to North Vietnam's logistical support of the war in South Vietnam was the panhandle. This monograph seeks to explain why this was so and to describe from the Laotian point of view the significant events of the conflict in Indochina which occured in the panhandle of Laos.

The Laos Panhandle

When we speak of the Laos panhandle, we are referring to that part of the country that extends south from about the 18th parallel and forms the corridor between Thailand's Korat Plateau and the narrow waist of Vietnam. Not only is the nation of Laos shaped like a key, but the shaft of the key — the panhandle — became the key to North Vietnam's successful prosecution of the war against the South.

Map 1 — The Key Position of Laos in Indochina

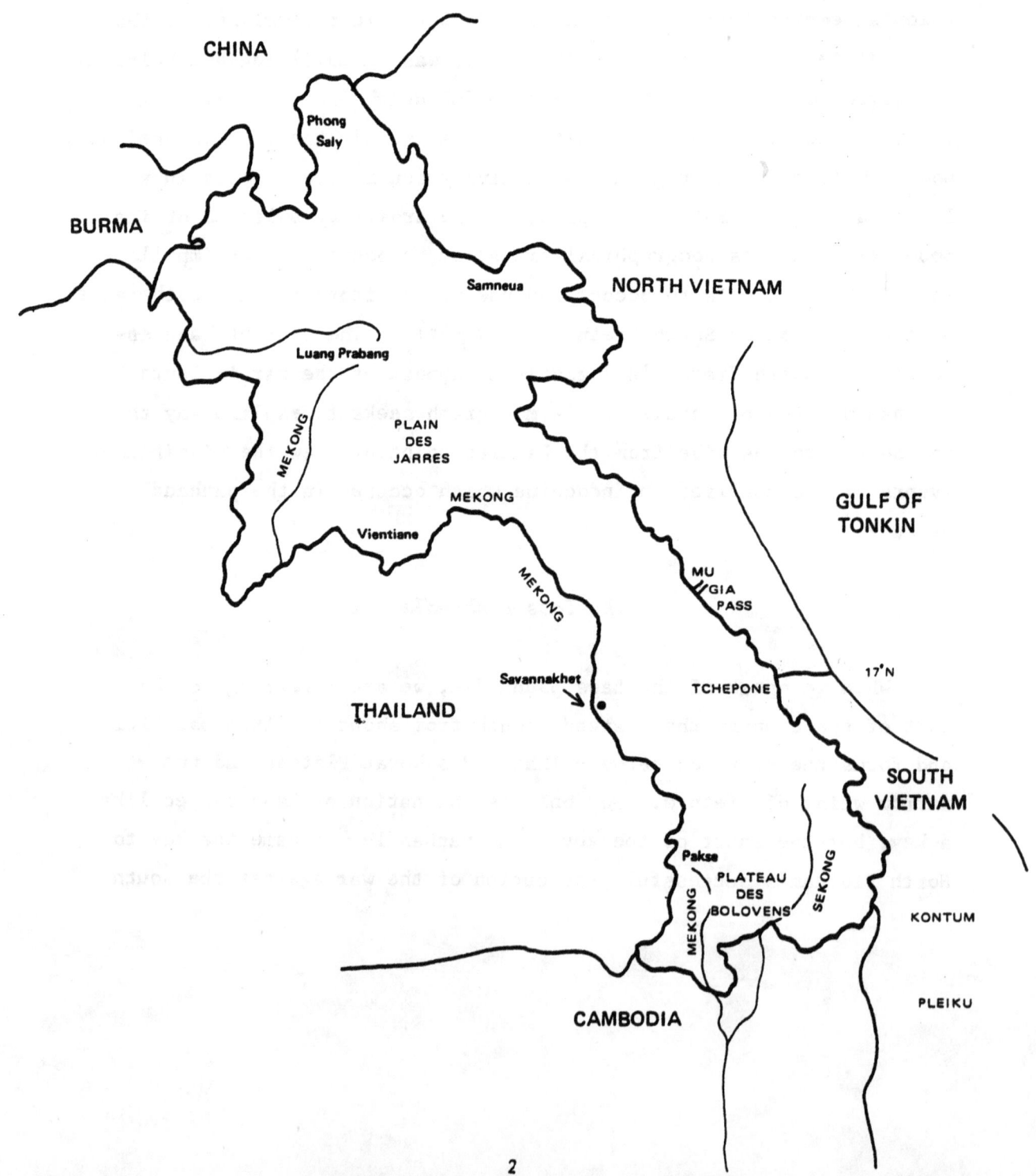

The Annamite chain runs along the entire eastern side of Laos. The chain extends northeast to southeast, paralleling the direction of flow of the Mekong River. In its upper portion, the mountains resemble those in northern Laos, having rugged peaks and deep valleys. The peaks are from approximately 5,000 to 8,000 feet in elevation and this portion of the chain presents a formidable barrier to movement between Laos and North Vietnam. In central-east Khammouane Province, the elevations are somewhat lower and passes allow easier crossing. Farther south, at about the latitude of the city of Khammouane, the chain enters a limestone region characterized by steep ridges and peaks, sink holes, and disappearing streams. Then, on a line roughly parallel with the Demilitarized Zone between North and South Vietnam, a comparatively flat area occurs and travel is relatively easy through this area. From this point to the southern end of Laos the chain again becomes very rugged and its elevations rise to 6,000 feet; the highest point is over 7,000 feet.

At the neck of the panhandle section the Annamite chain extends to the Mekong River. Below this section, mountains are buttressed on the west by several plateaus, the best known being the Cammon Plateau in Khammouane Province. From the rolling plain on the plateau, the land slopes gently westward to the alluvial plains along the Mekong River. Prominent in the southern part of the country is the fertile Bolovens Plateau. Almost encircled by a high escarpment, the plateau has an elevation of about 4,000 feet. Its terrain is also generally rolling and there are large patches of grassland.

Aside from the ruggedness of the terrain in the panhandle, the weather was the other significant factor which influenced military activity there. The midsummer rains that swept across Indochina, carried by the southwest monsoon, drenched the land with some of the heaviest rainfalls recorded anywhere in the world. The consequence was that all activity slowed during the summer months as the North Vietnamese reduced the traffic on the Ho Chi Minh trail and pulled their forces and temporary installations eastward toward the South

Vietnam border. As fall approached with the annual dry season, they again pushed westward in the panhandle and resumed the flow of traffic on the trails and roads of southern Laos.

The Ho Chi Minh Trail

Infiltration of Communist cadre from North to South Vietnam started in 1959 when the North Vietnamese decided to support and strengthen the guerrilla war in the South. They crossed the 17th parallel by two main routes: down the South China Sea in fishing boats, junks, and freighters; or through the mountainous jungles of the panhandle of Laos on foot, elephants, and bicycles. They used old paths through the mountains, the former colonial routes, and trails in the jungle that had been constructed during the Indochina war. This system of roads, trails and waterways became known as the Ho Chi Minh trail. In the beginning, the Ho Chi Minh trail served merely as a line of communication for Communist couriers and small combat units but they began making fuller use of it by 1962.

The trail runs through tropical, dense forests. The land is rugged and harsh even for the montagnards who inhabit it and exist under conditions that have not changed much since the stone age. The jungles along these trails are almost impenetrable primeval forests; the mountains are steep and rocky. During the French colonial regime, as well as after Laos independence, this part of the country was so remote, isolated and undeveloped that no effort was made to control it. But it was ideally suited for guerrilla warfare.

The distance from the Red River Delta in North Vietnam to the populous rice lands of the Mekong Delta in South Vietnam was shorter by way of Laos than by the road along the coast, even if use of the latter had been available to the Communists after the 1954 partition.

The passes across the Annamite Mountains between Vietnam and Laos are at relatively low elevations but approaches to these passes are through a wide strip of rugged terrain deeply cut by torrents and forested with thick jungle. Roads had to be engineered under most difficult conditions.

In the north sector, the North Vietnamese were able to use old roads through the Keo Neua and Mu Gia passes which had been improved during 1961 and 1962 under their aid agreements with Prince Souvannaphouma. In the southern sector, however, which ran through the area with the heaviest annual rainfall in Laos, new roads had to built. *(Map 2)*

This trail continues into the southern portion of South Vietnam and although it was referred to in the singular, it actually comprised a whole network of paths which could be used or abandoned as attempts at interdiction dictated. Many portions of the trail passed under thick tall trees, making it difficult or impossible to see from the air. In some sections waterways, such as the Sekong river that runs from A Shau through Banbac and Attopeu east of Bolovens Plateau, form part of the network. Activity along the trail varied with the seasons; traffic was heaviest during the dry season, October to May, and was lightest during the rainy season. *(Map 3)* The NVA moved materiel down the trail by stages and it was concealed in depot storage, rest and repair areas all along the way. Most transportation was by truck convoys but bicycles and foot porterage were employed when the need arose. Damaged sections of the trail were repaired rapidly and efficiently. *(Map 4)*

During the French domination of Indochina a French commission studied the feasibility of building a railroad from Dong Ha, Vietnam, to Savannakhet, but they later decided it would make sense to link Thakhek, Laos with Vietnam through Mu Gia pass because of the exportable tin that was close to Thakhek. Although this link was never completed, pylons for an aerial tramway were erected through the Mu Gia pass to bring construction supplies into the interior.

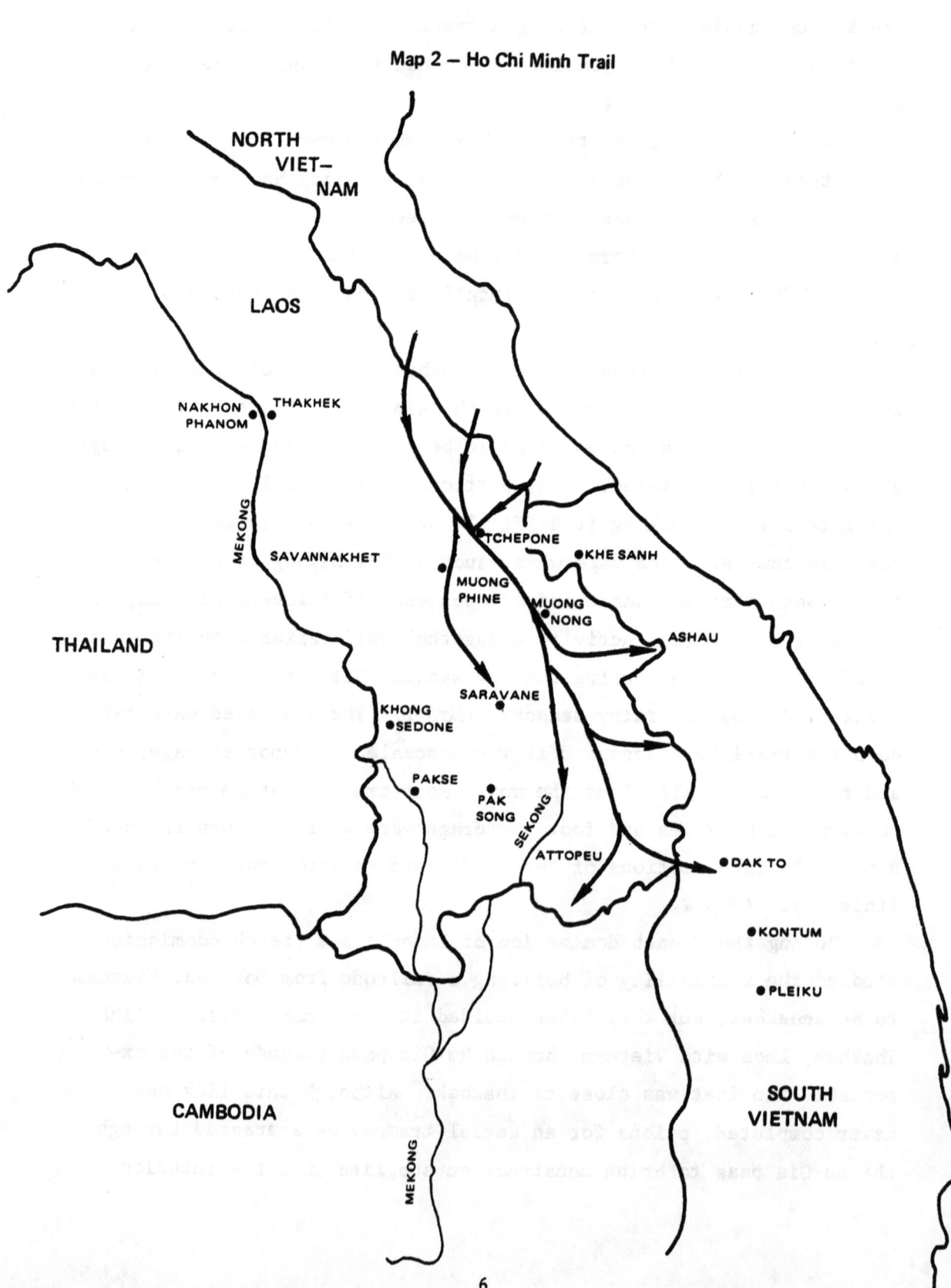

Map 2 — Ho Chi Minh Trail

Map 3 — Annual Rainfall In Laos

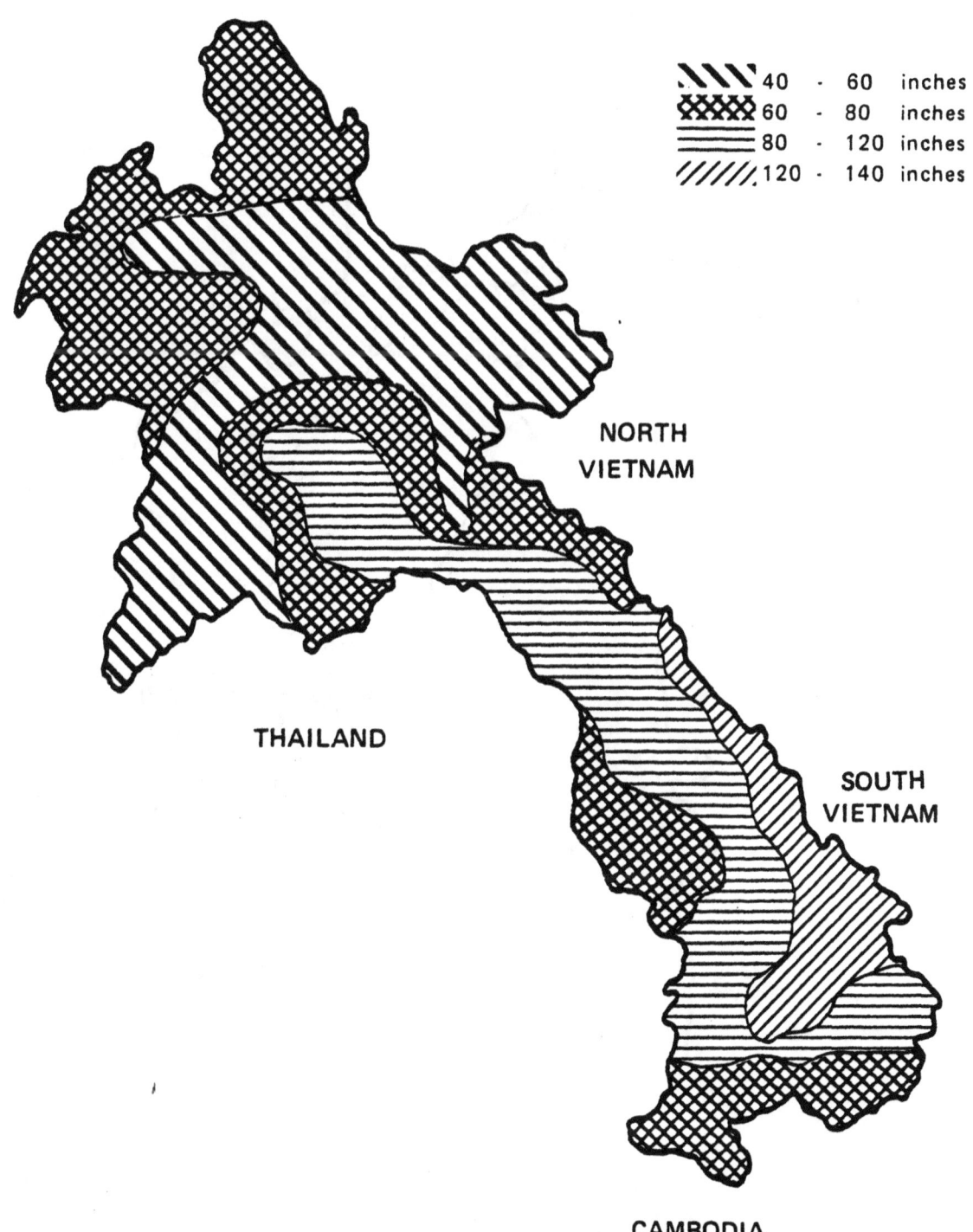

The governor-general of Indochina also spoke fondly of extending the motorable road existing then from Savannakhet to Muong Phine, near Tchepone, with Dong Ha, but budgetary constraints made such an enterprise impossible at that time. Following the March 9, 1945 *Coup*, the Viet Minh clamped their hold on the Tchepone region and its people. The French were preoccupied at this time with driving rebels out of Savannakhet and when they finally had time to turn their attention to Tchepone, the Viet Minh had already burned the house of the French district officer to the ground. The Tchepone region is at the geographic center of Indochina and its location gives it military importance. The routes used by the Viet Minh forces during their withdrawal from the central highlands of South Vietnam, from Cambodia, and from Southern Laos after the 1954 armistice went through Tchepone. As they moved northward they left behind caches of arms, some buried and some hidden in caves. These hiding points became the base area complex for the Second Indochina War (1956-1975) the war between North and South Vietnam. *(Map 5)* These base areas were used as depot or storage facilities for supplies and war materials such as POL, spare parts, ammunition, weapons, food and medicine, until it was feasible to move them on to South Vietnam or Cambodia. The NVA provided strong security and good camouflage to avoid damage by air and ground attacks since it would have been impossible to continue the war in the South without the trail network and the base areas along the Ho Chi Minh trail.

There were seven large base areas along the Ho Chi Minh trail in the panhandle; the five most important to support of NVA forces in South Vietnam were:

    Base Area 604 - Tchepone[1]
    Base Area 611 - East of Muong Nong
    Base Area 612 - Between Sarvane and Ban Bac

---

[1] This numbering of the base areas was done by the US/SVN combined intelligence staffs for convenience of identification. The NVA assigned names to the base areas.

Map 5 — The Enemy Base Area Complex in Eastern Mr III and Mr IV

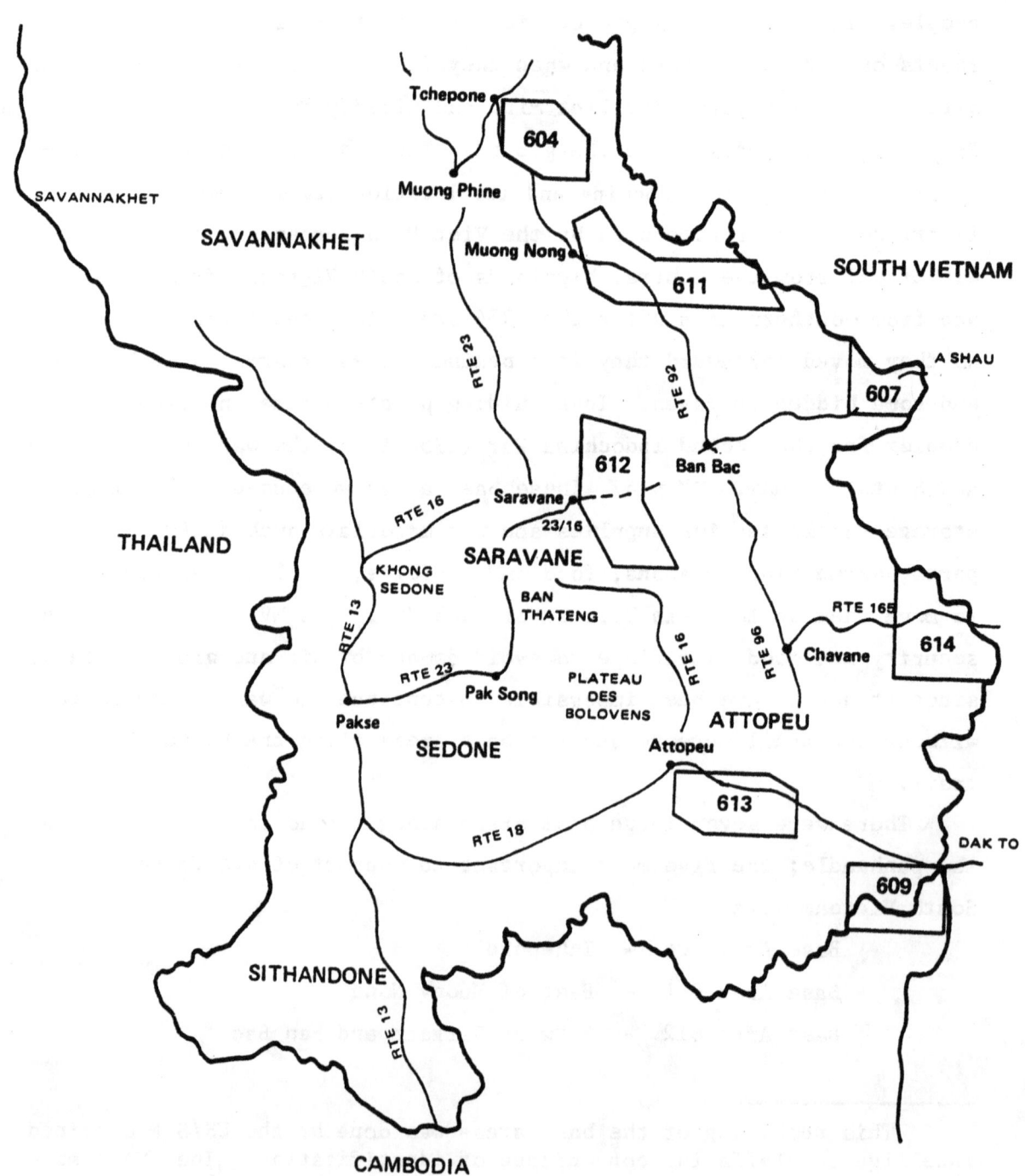

Heavily Camouflaged NVA Storage Bunker on the Ho Chi Minh Trail near Tchepone in the Laos panhandle

Base Area 614 — East of Chavane

Base Area 609 — Eastern Attopeu Province in the tri-border area of Cambodia, Vietnam and Laos

Base Area 604 was the main logistic base during the Vietnam War; from here the coordination and distribution of supplies into RVN Military Region 1 and to the base areas further to the south were accomplished.

Base Area 611 facilitated the transportation of supplies from Base Area 604 south to 609. Base Area 611 had fuel storage sites and fuel pipelines to supply Base Area 609 and the supply convoys moving in both directions. It also fed fuel and supplies to Base Area 607 and on into South Vietnam's A Shau Valley.

Base Area 612 was just as important as 604 and 611. It was used for logistic support of the enemy B-3 Front in the Vietnam central highlands.

Base Area 614 between Chavane, Laos, and Kham Duc, Vietnam was used primarily to transport war materials to South Vietnam's lowlands in RVN Military Region 2 and to the enemy B-3 Front.

Base Area 609 was important because of the fine road conditions that made it possible to move supplies to the B-3 Front when weather was bad and during the rainy season. Furthermore, the POL pipeline system completed in 1974 passed through this base area into South Vietnam.

Base Area 613, near Attopeu, primarily supported NVA forces in southern Laos and Cambodia.

The NVA logistical units, the Binh Trams, were under the control of the 559th Transportation Group.[2] Most main Binh Trams were composed of engineer, transportation, medical, anti-aircraft and infantry units. The Binh Trams provided gasoline for the convoys and food for the troops infiltrating into South Vietnam.

There were no Pathet Lao units authorized to operate along the infiltration corridor, and the local tribes were excluded from the area.

The North Vietnamese ran the Ho Chi Minh trail as if it were

---

[2] Freely translated "Binh Tram" meant "Commo-Liaison Site."

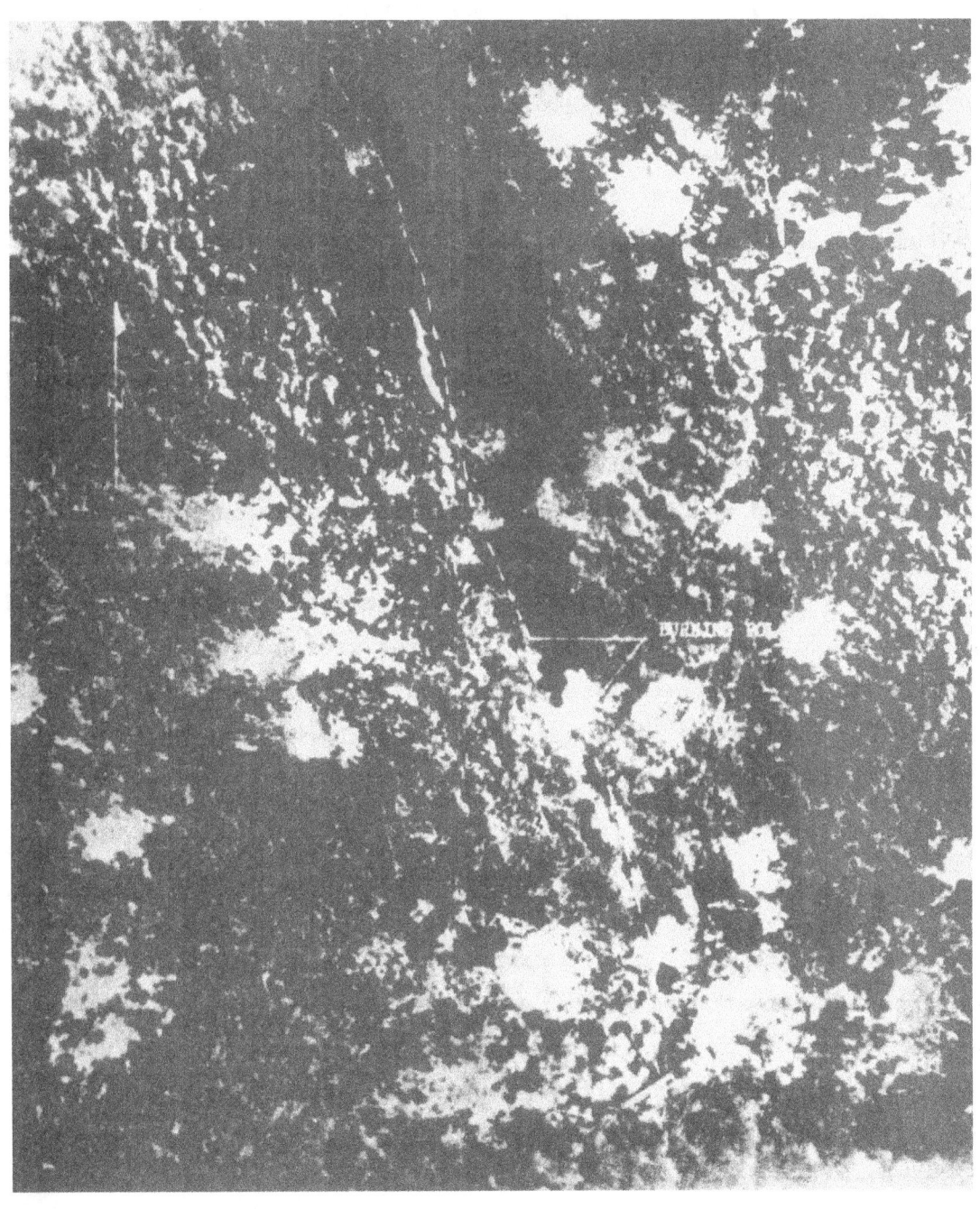

North Vietnamese Petroleum Pipe Line in the Laos Panhandle
The installation was under air attack at the time this photo was taken
(probably in 1972)

a strategic rear area of South Vietnam. NVA engineer units maintained the existing roads and built new ones. They also built the storage areas along the trail. Vietnamese labor battalions, including women, kept roads, paths, and storage areas in good repair. Vietnamese medical personnel maintained infirmaries along the routes to treat infiltrators and locally assigned Vietnamese. To provide some distraction from the arduous life of the Vietnamese stationed along the trail, entertainment troupes passed through from time to time with presentations of patriotic plays and songs.

The Vietnamese infiltrators were trucked through North Vietnam late at night and continued their difficult journey on foot once they had reached Laos. They marched day and night along well camouflaged trails. The infiltration groups ranged from small squads of specialists to units of five hundred troops. The large groups were fresh replacements destined to replace losses in units fighting in South Vietnam and to form new combat and logistical units there. The Binh Trams provided guides to lead them south.

The Sihanouk Trail

The Sihanouk trail was an extension of the Ho Chi Minh trail and branched off southeast of the Bolovens Plateau, south of Attopeu and Muong May. (Map 6) At the time the NVA started building the Sihanouk trail in 1965 in Attopeu Province, nobody knew, not even Colonel Khong Vongnarath who was commander of Attopeu Province, that the explosions of dynamite day and night were from the NVA construction near by and Colonel Khong was not inclined to investigate. NVA security was strong and Khong had a tacit understanding with the NVA to the effect that his patrols would not range far from the limits of Attopeu Town and NVA forces would not shell or otherwise interfere with his garrison. From time to time Colonel Khong would send soldiers disguised as elephant hunters into the NVA-controlled area around Attopeu and they would return with reports of NVA strength and activity, but no regular patrols were dispatched nor was any aggressive action

Map 6 – Sihanouk Trail

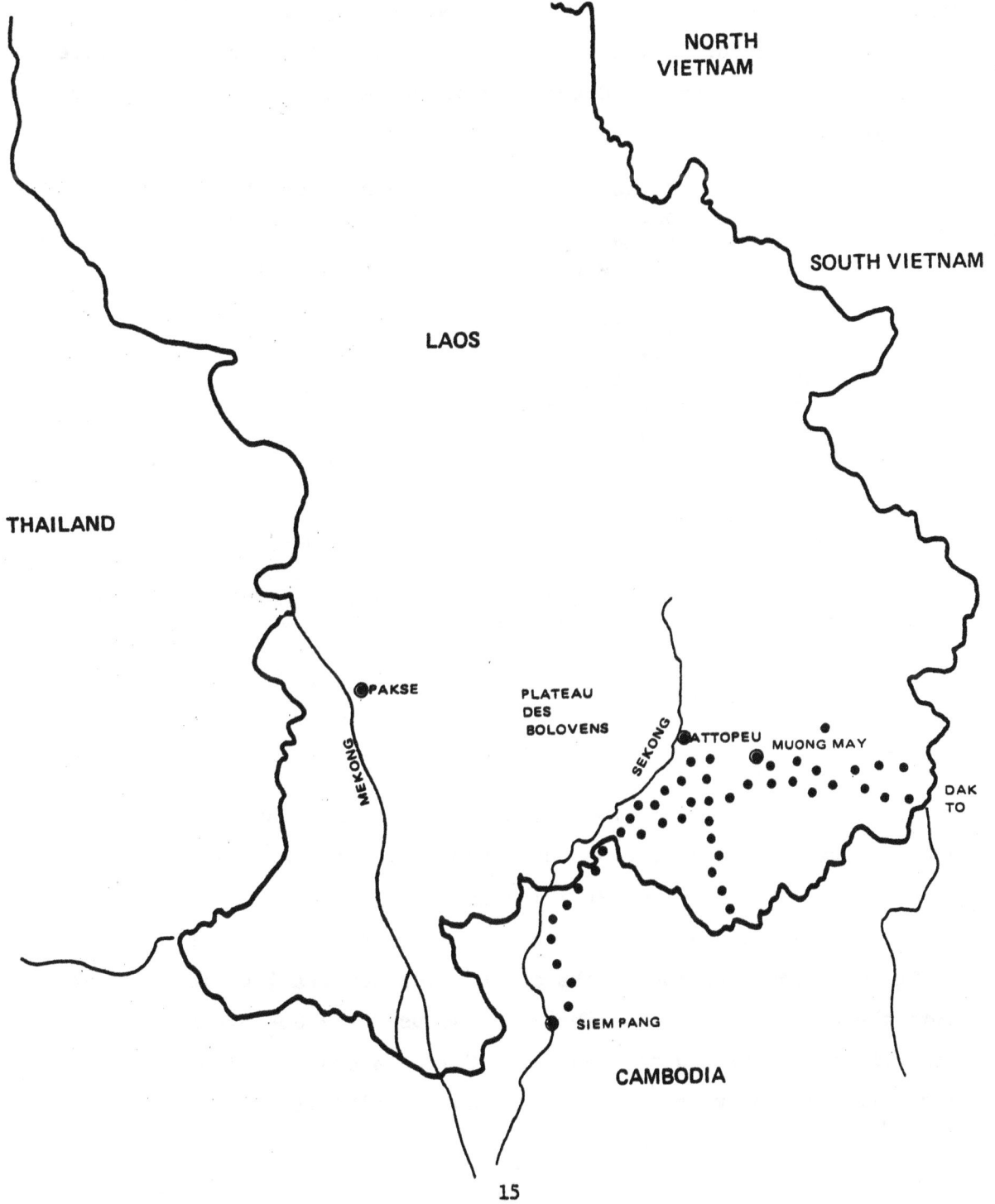

taken against the NVA. The danger of NVA retaliation was too great as was the potential loss of some lucrative commercial enterprises.

As the fighting in South Vietnam grew more intense the trail became a major military issue, perhaps a key issue in determining the outcome of the war. The flow of troops, weapons, and ammunition from north to south through Laos was constantly on the increase. Prince Sihanouk had allowed the Viet Cong and North Vietnamese to occupy the northeastern part of Cambodia. In a press conference in Peking, after he had been deposed by his Defense Minister, General Lon Nol, Sihanouk complained:

> "We had no neutrality. Now we are a colony of the Americans and are occupied by 65,000 South Vietnamese troops, mercenaries of Americans. I was deposed on March 18, 1970, because it was said that I allowed {Viet Cong and Viet Minh to occupy Cambodia}. They sometimes did come to Cambodia because of some necessity, some strategic or tactical necessity. But this was within the framework or their fight against the United States, to liberate their homeland."

> "Even if they were in Cambodia, they looked toward Saigon. All their efforts were directed toward Saigon and South Vietnam, they wanted to liberate South Vietnam, they never looked in our direction. They recognized *de jure* our frontiers; even in the future, after their victory, they cannot change the frontiers of Cambodia."

The NVA opened the Sihanouk trail in May 1966 and from that time on supplies began flowing into northern Cambodia. The NVA also used motor boats for shipping down the Sekong River to the Cambodia border. Laotian soldiers at the observation posts on the high ground along the rim of the Bolovens Plateau could hear the noise of the boats along the Sekong and the trucks on the Sihanouk trail could be heard from the Attopeu garrison. The NVA also used the Sekong to float bags of rice covered with plastic to Cambodia day and night. Trucks generally did not move at all when U.S. or RLAF aircraft were active and when they did move, they were always camouflaged with branches tied to frames covering the body of the truck. The drivers were experts at seeking cover during air raids or while observation or reconnaissance planes were overhead. They would hide under rock overhangs or in thickets. Since bridges became targets, underwater ramps were constructed of logs and stones, and for crossing wide rivers, bamboo rafts were kept moored to the banks, hidden by the overhanging trees. In some places stream beds were used for roadways to avoid telltale tracks. By 1970, all sections of the trail were protected by anti-aircraft guns, some with radar.

To protect the trail as it passed Attopeu, the NVA periodically harassed the RLG garrison there, firing mortars into the city and attacking forward positions. This was sufficient to discourage the Laos command from attempting any serious interference with NVA activity on the Sihanouk trail.

The Pathet Lao

As time passed, the North Vietnamese proved repeatedly that they possessed the military power to control the panhandle of Laos to the extent necessary to operate their extensive logistical and replacement system, but this capability was enhanced by their exploitation of the indigenous Communist movement in Laos.

The term Pathet Lao was first used in 1949 by those Lao forces that followed the Viet Minh lead and refused to accept accommodations with the French to which other Lao nationalists had acceded the previous year. The term gained international recognition when it was used at the Geneva Conference of 1954, although representatives of the PL forces were not seated at the conference and it was a Viet Minh general who signed the cease-fire with the French on their behalf. The name remained in common use as a generic term for the Lao Communists despite the fact that a legal political party, the Neo Lao Hak Sat (NLHS), the Lao Patriotic Front, was formed in early 1956. Therefore, although Pathet Lao was properly the name only for the armed forces of the Lao Communists between 1950 and 1965, it was used colloquially and included all non-Vietnamese components of the Laos Communist movement and has continued in use to this day. Other names used were Phak Pasason Lao (PPL) the People's Party of Laos, a semi-secret Communist Party organization; the Lao People's Liberation Army (LPLA), the Kong Thap Potpoy Pasason Lao, which were the armed forces under the command of the NLHS Central Committee; and the Dissident Neutralists (or Patriotic Neutralist Forces).

From about 1965 until the cease-fire there were six Pathet Lao battalions in Military Region IV, the southern end of the panhandle. Each of the provinces of Saravane, Attopeu, Champassak, Sithandone, Sedone, and Vapikham Thong had one battalion. The strength of a battalion varied from 150 to 300 men but frequently they existed at only cadre-strength and were dispersed in small units.

The Pathet Lao units lived with the population in the villages and they wore civilian clothes most of the time. Their mission was to ambush the supply lines of the Royal Laos Army (RLA) and conduct light harassing attacks against the RLA positions. Dispersed in small units, they had to assemble for operations. The PL cadres levied rice, pork, and chicken in the local areas for the NVA. They also recruited young men and sent them to northern Laos for training as soldiers and to be equipped with new weapons such as the AK-47 automatic rifle, submachine guns, 60-mm and 82-mm mortars. The PL units had modern weapons as good as those used by the NVA, but despite this modern armament, the PL were ineffective against RLG forces in the panhandle and required the constant support and guidance of the North Vietnamese.

Relations Between the Pathet Lao and the NVA

When the Vietnamese under Ho Chi Minh launched their anti-French independence movement, it was natural that they should have the support of certain Lao who had particularly close ties to the Vietnamese.

Future Lao Communist leaders Kaysone Phoumuihan and Nouhak Phomsavan, for example, and even some members of the Lao upper classes, including Prince Souphanouvong, Phoumi Vongvichit, and Singkapo Chounramany were ready to accept Vietnamese leadership in the making of their own revolution. The Vietnamese influenced the Lao revolutionaries, or perhaps one should say that the Lao revolutionaries willingly cooperated with and even subordinated themselves to the Vietnamese Communists. A widely accepted thesis holds that most Laotians dislike the Vietnamese but anti-Vietnamese feelings did not appear to be intense, although members of the Lao elite feared what they perceived as Vietnamese aggressiveness and organizational skill and, often betraying a sense of their own inferiority, they saw unfortunate implications for Laos in too close an association with the Vietnamese. The feeling of inadequacy *vis-a-vis* the Vietnamese was particularly evident among the educated Lao who had once been placed in positions subordinate to the Vietnamese by French colonial officers whose administrative policies tended to discriminate against the Lao.

Prince Souphanouvong visited Viet Minh headquarters in North Vietnam in 1949 and he was warmly welcomed by Ho Chi Minh. When the Viet Minh were reconstituted as the Lao Dong Party (Vietnamese Workers' Party), Prince Souphanouvong attended the first Party congress in February 1951, as did a number of other Lao and Cambodian observers.

The congress produced a platform containing the following significant clauses:

> The people of Vietnam must unite closely with the people of Laos and Cambodia and give them every assistance in the common struggle against imperialist aggression, for the complete liberation in Indochina and the defense of world peace.
>
> In the common interest of the three peoples, the people of Vietnam are willing to enter into long term cooperation with the peoples of Laos and Cambodia, with a view to bringing about an independent, strong and prosperous federation of the states of Vietnam, Laos and Cambodia if the three peoples so desire.

After Laos gained independence at the Geneva conference in 1954 it soon became evident that the Pathet Lao had no intention of limiting their struggle for power to mere participation in Vientiane politics; to competing with other political groups within the framework of the existing political system. While engaging in cautious negotiations with the RLG they sought to consolidate their control over the two provinces of Samneua and Phong Saly, which had been designated by the conference as regroupment zones for their military forces prior to integration into the National Army. At the same time, the Pathet Lao began to build their own political and administrative institutions in the two northern provinces so as to have a permanent base for future advances into other areas. In the panhandle, however, the Pathet Lao went underground, just as the Viet Cong did in South Vietnam after the 1954 agreement.

Significant Developments Following the 1962 Geneva Agreement

The Second Indochina War started after the French were defeated in the battle in Dien Bien Phu in North Vietnam in 1954 and the Geneva agreements failed to achieve a solution to the Vietnam problem. The objective of North Vietnam in the Second Indochina War was to take over South Vietnam and control all of Indochina, including Laos and Cambodia, and the 1962 Geneva Accords had no deterrent effect on North Vietnam's determination to accomplish this objective. This monograph attempts to explain how and why the panhandle of Laos became a battleground in North Vietnam's conquest of South Vietnam and Cambodia, even though the world paid little attention to the forgotten war in Laos.

In my opinion, there were six significant events following the 1962 accords that more than others influenced the course of the war in the panhandle of Laos. First among these, chronologically, was the departure of United States military advisers who had contributed so much to the modernization of the RLA. They were replaced at headquarters levels by a few American civilians, but the vital work the American Army officers and noncommissioned officers were doing in the field was no longer done.

Second, motivated by a number of related factors, the North Vietnamese vastly increased their commitment of regular forces in Laos, particularly in the panhandle, totally ignoring the prohibitions contained in the 1962 accords. These reinforcements, in combat as well as logistical units, constructed, operated, and protected the complex logistical system through southern Laos that the NVA required to support its heavy and growing expeditionary force in South Vietnam. US and South Vietnamese air and naval operations along the coast of South Vietnam gradually became more effective in intercepting North Vietnamese seaborne contraband traffic into the South, forcing even greater reliance on the land line of communications through Laos.

The third major event was the Cambodian change of government in 1970 which shifted that nation's policy from one of accommodation toward the Communists to one of reliance on US tactical and logistical support. This event closed the Cambodian ports to North Vietnamese supply ships that were moving great quantities of military materiel through Cambodia to the NVA and Viet Cong forces in the southern battlefields of South Vietnam. The closure of the ports meant that nearly all logistical support of the NVA in South Vietnam had to come through Laos, again increasing the importance of the Ho Chi Minh and Sihanouk trail systems and making it imperative that the flow not be interrupted. Not only was the system through southern Laos essential to logistical support of the NVA in South Vietnam, but virtually all replacements and new units made the march from North Vietnam to South Vietnam through the Laos panhandle. The great NVA offensives of 1968, 1969, and 1972, with their unprecedented casualties, required a steady flow of fresh replacements who could only reach the battlefields through the Laos panhandle.

A fourth event which impelled the NVA to take even more vigorous actions to protect the trail system through south Laos was the South Vietnamese raid-in-force into the heart of the Ho Chi Minh trail system at Tchepone in early 1971. This operation, Lam Son 719, contributed to South Vietnamese and Cambodian objectives, but certainly made it clear to the NVA that the system was vulnerable and had to be secured at all costs. The NVA continued to expand the system westward onto the Plateau de Bolovens, nearly to the Mekong River itself.

The 1973 Paris agreement to end the war in South Vietnam, and the similar agreement signed the following month pertaining to Laos were collectively the fifth event which significantly altered the course of the war in the panhandle. These agreements withdrew all US combat support from the RLA and meant also that the US would no longer interdict the Ho Chi Minh trail in southern Laos. The NVA then had free, uninhibited use of the system in the panhandle. The RLA and the Laos irregulars withdrew from all forward bases and no longer even offered token harrassment to the NVA. Furthermore, the new neutralist government of Laos reduced its armed forces to less than one fourth its former size, while the Pathet Lao, backed up by the NVA, grew ever stronger.

By the time of the final significant event, the collapse of South Vietnam on 30 April 1975, the Communists were in position to exploit the weakness of the loyal government forces. This was the final chapter, written as the Pathet Lao, in May 1975, streamed into the national and provincial capitals and forcefully asserted its supremacy. The people of Laos had lost their quest for neutrality, and their country had become a vassal state of their strong, red neighbors, the North Vietnamese.

CHAPTER II

The Organization and Employment
of Irregular Forces in Southern Laos

The Military Regions

Laos was divided into five military regions two of which were located in the panhandle. *(Map 7)* Military Region I at Luang Prabang was dominated by the royal family and the former commander in Chief of the Royal Laos Army, General Oune Rathikul. The region commander was Brigadier General Tiao Sayavong, a half brother of the king. The region was located in northwest Laos and covered four provinces: Phong Saly, Houa Khong, Sayaboury and Luang Prabang.

Military Region II, in the northeastern section of Laos, was under Major General Vang Pao, the Meo guerrilla war hero of Laos. It covered two provinces: Houa Phan (Samneua), and Xieng Khouang. The headquarters was at Long Cheng, northwest of the Plain of Jars.

Military Region III in central Laos was headquartered at Savannakhet and covered two provinces; Khammouane (Thakhek) and Savannakhet. This region was commanded by General Bounpon and later by Brigadier General Nouphet Dao Heuang, in July 1971. The real power in this region was the Insixiengmay family led by Minister Leuam Insixiengmay, Vice Premier and Minister of Education.

Military Region IV, with headquarters at Pakse, included the six provinces of southern Laos: Saravane, Attopeu, Champassak, Sedone, Khong Sedone, and Sithandone (Khong Island). It was dominated by the Nachampassak family led by Prince Boun Oum Nachampassak. The commander of Military Region IV was Major General Phasouk S. Rassaphak, a member of the Champassak family. He commanded this area for almost a decade and a half until finally replaced by the author, Brigadier General Soutchay Vongsavanh, in July 1971.

Map 7 – Indochina Military Regions

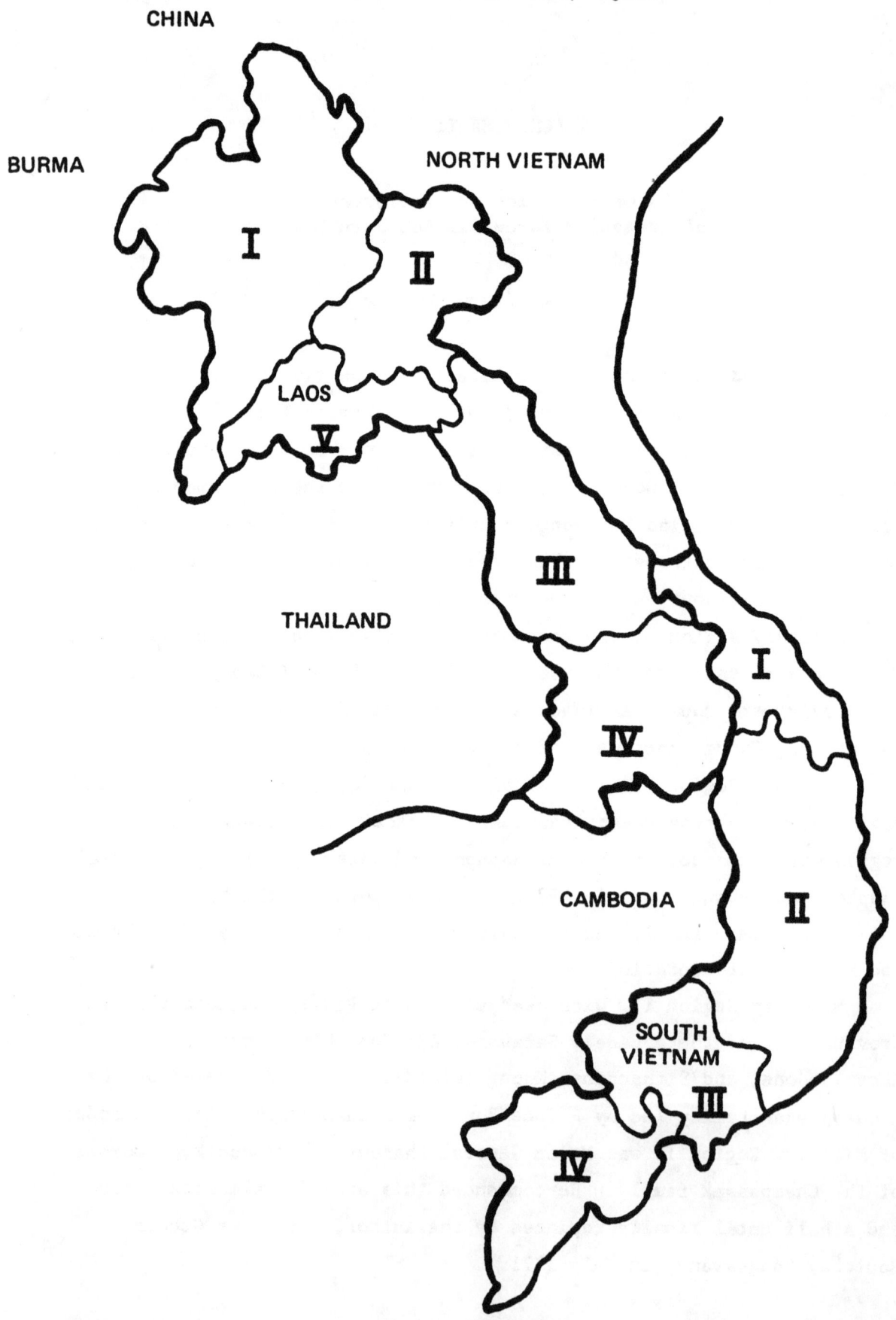

Military Region V contained Borikhane and Vientiane Provinces, the capital province of Laos, was headquartered at Chinaimo Army Camp and was led by Major General Kouprasith Abhay until he was replaced by Brigadier General Thongligh Chokbeng Boun in July 1971.

While I was Chief of Staff for guerrilla forces in Military Region IV, I was frequently called upon to present briefings to headquarters visitors on the military situation in the region. In order to clarify the complex nature of relative security in the southern panhandle, I estimated the areas under the *de facto* control of the opposing forces and illustrated the situation on the map. In mid-1970, zones of control were recognized in this manner as Zone I, or the west zone, from the Thailand border to the east, controlled by the Royal Lao Army; Zone II, or the central zone, was the contested zone; and Zone III, or the east zone, from the South Vietnam border to the west, was controlled by the North Vietnamese Army (NVA). *(Map 8)* Most of the Ho Chi Minh trail was located in eastern Zone II and along the boundary between Zones II and III.

Interdiction of the NVA Logistics System in the Panhandle

The panhandle of Laos indeed carried the life-blood of the NVA expeditionary force in South Vietnam. Recognizing this, but denied by observance of the 1962 accords the freedom to block the Laos supply corridor with the large infantry formations that would be required, the U.S. and South Vietnam undertook to interdict the trail from the air and through the use of small teams of raiders. As sophisticated and effective as some of the weapons and techniques were, and some were truly devastating in their local effects, none achieved the goal of seriously impeding the flow of men and equipment south. As viewed by the author and discussed in Chapter III even the audacious attack of the South Vietnamese into Tchepone in early 1971 failed to have lasting impact. The attack came years too late, and the force was too small and too lightly supported. But it confirmed for all to see that the Ho Chi Minh trail was a vital area to the North Vietnamese and reinforced, without serious

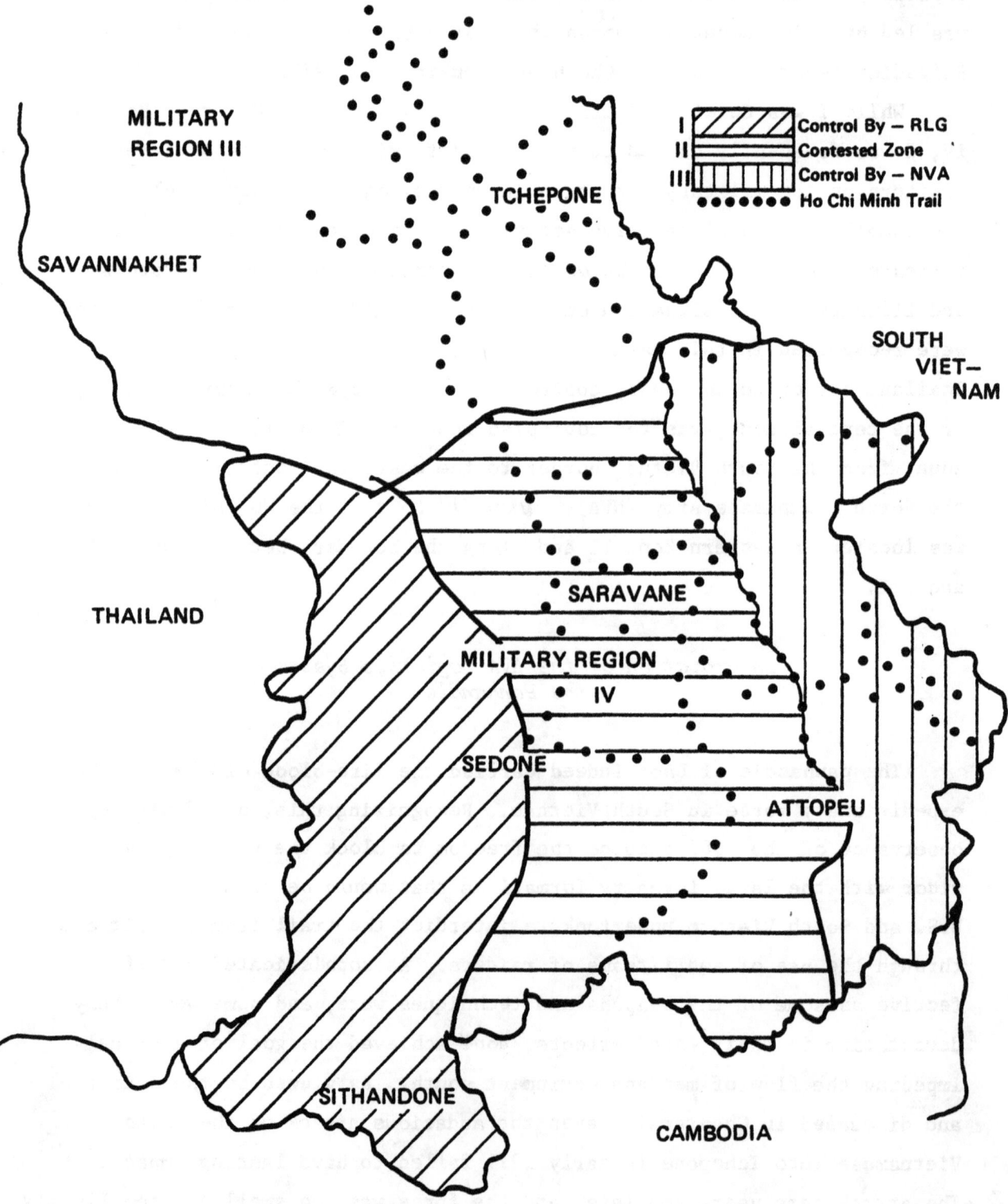

Map 8 – Zones of Control and the Ho Chi Minh Trail

question, the theory that only the complete blockage of this route could force the North to suspend, if not abandon, its conquest of South Vietnam. It also clearly illustrated the truth that Laos could not be neutral. North Vietnam would never permit it, since true neutrality for Laos would deny the use of its territory for aggression. Tragically, for Laos, South Vietnam, and Cambodia, the United States persisted in its fundamental policy of refusing to upset the 1962 accords to the extent required to sever permanently the Ho Chi Minh trail.

Laos armed forces involvement in air interdiction attempts began in October 1964 with occasional raids by the Royal Laos Air Force (RLAF) T-28s but in 1969 these had to stop because of the effectiveness of the NVA anti-aircraft artillery. Besides, most movement of troops and supplies was conducted during the night when aerial bombing was ineffective.

Following the change of government in Cambodia in 1970, US air efforts against the trail systems increased enormously and the trail defenders steadily increased their anti-aircraft fire in response. The anti-aircraft units had the advantage of knowing when the trucks would be moving, and slower aircraft, such as gunships, forward air control (FAC) planes, and helicopters were relatively easy targets for them. Before 1970, the NVA hid their anti-aircraft guns and would not fire at airplanes in order to remain concealed. After 1970, however, they fired at any plane in range.

Several thousand NVA engineering troops were responsible for upkeep and repair of the trail. The road-builders also built bomb shelters, repair facilities and areas for parking trucks. Gasoline and oil were pumped across the mountains through hidden pipelines and stored in drums to be dropped off at camp sites at regular intervals. Caves were used to conceal material. When the US Air Force bombed to crater the road, the North Vietnamese would build by-passes or fill in the craters. When portions of the road were concealed by large trees, 500 pound bombs were used to blast the trees into barriers, but the North Vietnamese had enough engineer troops and materials to quickly clear the obstacles.

The South Vietnamese had by far the greatest stake in the attempts to stop the NVA use of the Ho Chi Minh trail in the panhandle. While

Camouflaged storage bunker on the Ho Chi Minh trail in the Laos Panhandle. A road-widening bulldozer has cut into the bank revealing the hidden entrance and destroying a bicycle

the greatest weight of the interdiction effort was carried out by the
U.S. Air Force, the South Vietnamese conducted a clandestine campaign
on the ground against trail installations and traffic.

One might expect that since Laos, Cambodia and South Vietnam were
each engaged in a war for their survival as free, independent, non-
Communist states against the enemy, North Vietnam, and each was supported by the same great power, the United States, that some extraordinary
and effective systems and procedures to coordinate the common effort for
the common good must have been devised by them and vigorously supported by the United States. Remarkably, and unfortunately, this was
not the case. There was virtually no coordination of combat activity
against the North Vietnamese, no communications between the armed
forces below the head-of-government level, and very little exchange
of information between them.

South Vietnamese Activities in the Panhandle

A link between the armies of Laos and the Republic of Vietnam
existed since the creation of the two armed forces. Both armies came
from the same source: the French Union Army. Many of the early
members, Laotian and Vietnamese, had served as officers, non-coms and
soldiers in the same French units during the colonial period. I graduated
from the officers' academy at Dong Hene, Savannakhet, and was commissioned
second lieutenant in 1953 and consequently had no early contact with
the Vietnamese military. Posted to a French-led battalion at Luang
Prabang, I was the only Lao platoon leader in my company; the company
commander and the other platoon leaders were French.

From 1954, when many tacit agreements were reached, high-level
military contact between the two armies continued. Liaison teams of
the Vietnamese Special Forces were authorized to enter Laos, mainly
around Vientiane, Thakhek, Savannakhet, and Pakse. Under Laos Armed
Forces cover, these teams freely operated to collect needed intelligence.

We were well aware that the South Vietnamese command was anxious to gather information concerning the NVA units that were passing through Laos to South Vietnam and were interested in information of the NVA operating in the panhandle. Information related to the NVA and the Viet Cong was collected by our service and passed to them. But the flow of information, at least insofar as I was concerned in MR IV, was one-way only. The Vietnamese kept a colonel, in civilian cover, at my headquarters in Pakse. He maintained close contact with my G-2 who passed him all intelligence of value concerning the NVA in southern Laos. But my G-2 received nothing in return that would help us against the NVA who opposed us in the panhandle. From time to time, NVA prisoners captured by our units asked to be passed to the South Vietnamese teams. These prisoners were released as requested because they were intelligence agents planted by the South Vietnamese in enemy units.

As military region commander, the only US-produced intelligence I received was through my American civilian adviser and the American military attache who from time to time passed me items of high interest, usually gained from sophisticated American sources such as photo and electronic reconnaissance.

But despite the willing cooperation demonstrated by the Laos Armed Forces there was a great lack of prior coordination practiced by South Vietnamese and their American advisers in operations in the Laos panhandle. Many South Vietnamese military operations were conducted without our knowledge. For example, the Vietnamese and US commands in the highlands would dispatch their troops on operations in Laos territory and later find that they needed our help in lifting supplies to them and for transporting the sick or wounded out of the area. We provided helicopters for these services, which we were happy to do, but we would have appreciated being advised in advance. All coordination in these matters was conducted between the Americans and the RLG in Vientiane. The military region commanders had no direct communications with South Vietnamese, nor did the units in the field ever exchange liaison officers. Consequently, there was no coordination of the combat effort in the field.

The biggest South Vietnamese operation in Laos was Lam Son 719, but the Laos military knew nothing about it until it happened. Then, radio sources and the press informed us only that a big South Vietnamese operation was taking place somewhere in the southern part of the Laotain countryside. Lam Son 719 took place during the period of neutrality when Laos had adopted a nonpartisan position *vis-a-vis* the Republic of Vietnam and the People's Republic of Vietnam. Laos had made it clear that it preferred to be left out of the struggle between the two Vietnams. Although this was the official political policy, the Laos military still maintained rapport with the South Vietnamese military and when Lam Son 719 started, Prime Minister Souvannaphouma, for the sake of form only, protested to the Republic of Vietnam's Government on the incursion. It was not until later that we in the army were briefed on the operation in our military area of responsibility.

Coordination between us and the South Vietnamese should have been better. We operated many irregular battalions along the Ho Chi Minh trail and had road watch teams observing NVA trucks and calling for air strikes, while at the same time other friendly military units were conducting the same type of operations; but there was no coordination of efforts. We estimated the number of operations conducted by units of the Vietnamese Army by the wounded that were carried out and the helicopters that landed in our zone.

Coordination between Cambodia and Laos in the Panhandle

Coordination between MR IV forces and the Cambodian forces was virtually non-existent. For that matter, there was little to coordinate because the Cambodians would not fight the NVA in the northern bordering provinces. We did offer the Cambodians some training support, but they didn't exploit it to much advantage.

Following the 1970 change of government in Cambodia, the new government, with the tacit agreement of RLA command, sent two battalions of recruits

A South Vietnamese Army Unit advances in the Laos panhandle near Tchepone in Operation Lam Son 719, February 1971

with their cadres, to train in MR IV at PS-18.[1] These new recruits received excellent training and were well motivated during their three months in Laos. After training, the two battalions were sent into combat on the Bolovens Plateau against the NVA. Here they were baptized by fire and identified as Battalion 601 and 602 but they did not fight well; their country had been at peace for a long time and their cadres, trained in the French Army tradition, knew more of theory than of practice. After two months against the NVA in the panhandle they were returned to Cambodia.

In order to maintain liaison with our headquarters, the Cambodian Army sent one colonel to stay in Sithandone Province. His duties included taking care of the Cambodia refugees and serving as Governor of Stung Streng Province as well as the brigade commander of northern Cambodia. He had approximately 300 men with him which he used to send reconnaissance teams into Cambodia to call for air strikes on supply depots or headquarters areas of the Khmer Rouge. But they had never clashed with the enemy in northern Cambodia. The commander appeared to be more interested in collecting information in Laos than in Cambodia, and although he often said that he planned to send the troops into Cambodia, he never did.

Laos Irregulars Before 1970

The concept of organizing, equipping and employing irregular, or guerrilla forces, in southern Laos was never originally considered by the Laos Military Region commanders in MR III or IV. The idea was totally American in its origin and was proposed by Americans to achieve the American objectives of interdicting the Ho Chi Minh trail, an objective that had no direct relationship to RLG security goals.

---

[1] PS-18 was an irregular operating base on the Bolovens Plateau. The letters stood for "Pakse Site," the principal city of the region and the location of headquarters, Military Region IV.

Laos Irregulars in Training at
an Irregular Base Camp on the Plateau des Bolovens Before 1970

Following the conclusion of the First Indochina War in 1954, the armed forces of Laos, in addition to the regular army, included local forces known as Auto Defence de Choc and Auto Defence Ordinaire. By 1968, most of these units had been dissolved and there were three categories of forces in the Royal Laos armed forces. First, the Battalion Volunteer (BV) which were located in each province with the mission of territorial defense; they coordinated with the local administration. Second, the Battalion Infantry (BI), which could be deployed to any of the provinces in the military region and could be sent out to reinforce in other regions. Third, the Special Guerrilla Units (SGU) or irregular forces who were paid by the Americans and used to fight anywhere in Laos.

There were two types of irregular forces in Military Region IV: the Special Guerrilla Unit Battalion (SGU-BN), successor to the Auto Defence de Choc, and the Guerrilla Battalion (GB), successor to the Auto Defence Ordinaire. The SGU-BN had five companies, a staff, and a strength of 550 men. Its mission was to conduct offensive operations and attack NVA and Pathet Lao positions in its zone. It operated on the Ho Chi Minh trail, in the enemy's logistical and security areas. SGU-BNs were also used to reinforce in other military regions. The GB consisted of five companies but never operated as a battalion. The companies were located close to their home villages and were employed to defend the villages. Local people were recruited for these battalions which were approximately 400 men strong. An additional mission of the GB was to support and reinforce the SGU-BN.

Each guerrilla zone had three battalions: one SGU-BN and two GB. The guerrilla zone commander also commanded the SGU-BN.[1] *(Chart 1)*

The RLA furnished the leaders for the guerrilla forces from the platoon leader to battalion commander and the guerrilla forces in Military Region IV were governed by the orders, regulations, and discipline of the Regular Army.

---

[1] Guerrilla Zones (GZ) are discussed on p. 39. There were three GZ in MR4 and each GZ commander was subordinate to the MR commander.

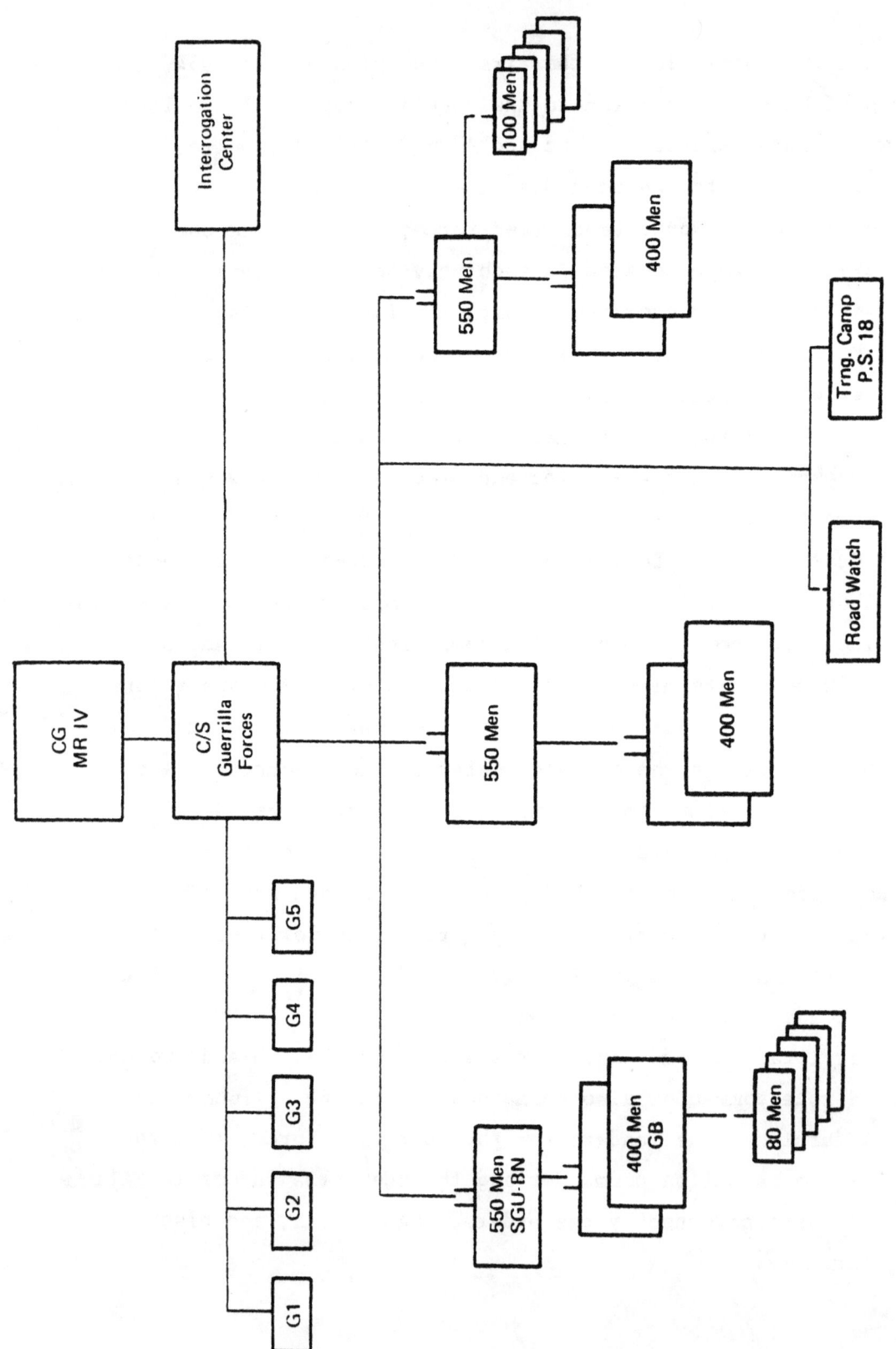

Chart 1 — The Irregular Organization in Military Region IV Before 1970

In 1958, the "Red Prince," Souphanouvong, when challenged with evidence that the NVA had sent two battalions of regular troops to occupy the village of Tchepone in the remote eastern panhandle, replied that this was of no great import because that terrain belonged to Vietnam anyway. While this never became the official RLG position concerning the eastern panhandle, the RLG leadership accepted the reality that it was quite powerless to eject or even interfere with the NVA troops in the panhandle. On the other hand, as it became more and more apparent to the Americans that the NVA was making crucial use of this region to prolong and escalate the war against South Vietnam, the Americans decided to do something about it.

We in Laos understood the difficulty the Americans and South Vietnamese faced. The U.S. was bound to observe the 1962 accords on Laos and could not interfere directly with the NVA in southern Laos. The U.S. had withdrawn, in 1962, all its military personnel except for the attache element in Vientaine. By 1964, the Americans began operations against the NVA logistics and infiltration system in southern Laos by infiltrating small teams of irregulars into the trail system to observe and report activity.

Gradually units of pure Lao composition were organized, and a series of bases -- eventually nine in all -- were established on the eastern rim of the Bolovens Plateau. From these bases raids were conducted against NVA convoys and installations on the Ho Chi Minh trail. The bases contained training areas, barracks, and communications and all eventually had to be fortified when the NVA reacted against them.

Throughout this early period neither the Royal Lao Government nor the Royal Lao Army had anything to do with the organization, equipping or operations of the Lao irregulars. They were supervised and paid exclusively by American civilians who also assigned them their missions. At this time, 1968, my groupement mobile was dissolved. The emphasis that had been placed on the organization of the irregular forces in the Laos armed forces had attracted most of the best officers and NCOs away from the regulars and as a result the groupement mobile had gradually become less and less combat effective. Furthermore, such large organizations under central authority were perceived by the top leadership in Vientiane as constant *coup* threats. Without a command, I was assigned as chief of staff of guerrilla forces in Military Region IV. I had been working closely with the guerrilla forces since 1967, while groupement mobile commander, and as General Phasouk's principal adviser and liaison officer with the irregulars.

In May 1967, early in my experience of coordinating irregular operations with the Americans in Military Region IV, a plan was developed to interdict the Ho Chi Minh trail east of the Bolovens Plateau. The primary purpose of the operation was to test the speed and effectiveness of the NVA response to a lodgement in this vital part of its trail system. Secondly, I and the Americans wanted to test the irregular forces in a company-sized, airmobile operation. Up to this time, they had operated only as squads and platoons. Thirdly, we wanted to test the procedures for the coordination of direct air support in his environment. The 100-man guerrilla company was loaded into Air America H-34 helicopters -- about 10 soldiers in each aircraft -- and it air-assaulted south of Chavane in the early morning hours.[2] The NVA reaction was indeed swift and violent. Before any air support could be employed against them, the NVA soldiers overran the position and 12 hours after landing, the company of Laos irregulars was wiped-out. Only 15 men escaped to return to battalion headquarters.

As the Lao irregular units grew in size and number, a greater amount of coordination and cooperation with RLA territorial commands and regular forces became a necessity. Consequently, as chief of staff for irregulars I designated guerrilla zones of operations and executed agreements between the irregulars and the regulars to define rules of coordination. In mid-1968, I divided the area of operations in Military Region IV into three guerrilla zones: *(Map 9)*

Guerrilla Zone I was located between latitude 15° and 15° 30' and from the South Vietnam frontier to the Thailand frontier. It included the Ho Chi Minh trail around Chavane, and its main base was located at PS-22, east of the Bolovens Plateau.

Guerrilla Zone II was south of Zone I, between latitude 15° and the Cambodia frontier. It included the Sihanouk Trail, Attopeu, Muong May, and the Mekong River. The base was located at PS-38 southeast of Bolovens Plateau.

Guerrilla Zone III was north of Zone I, between latitude 15° 30' and the boundary of Military Region III in Saravane Province and included the Ho Chi Minh trail from Ban Bac to the north and east. The base was located at PS-39, east of Saravane.

---

[2] Air America was the U.S. contract carrier in Indochina, civilian-manned.

Map 9 — The Guerrila Zones In Military Region IV Before 1970

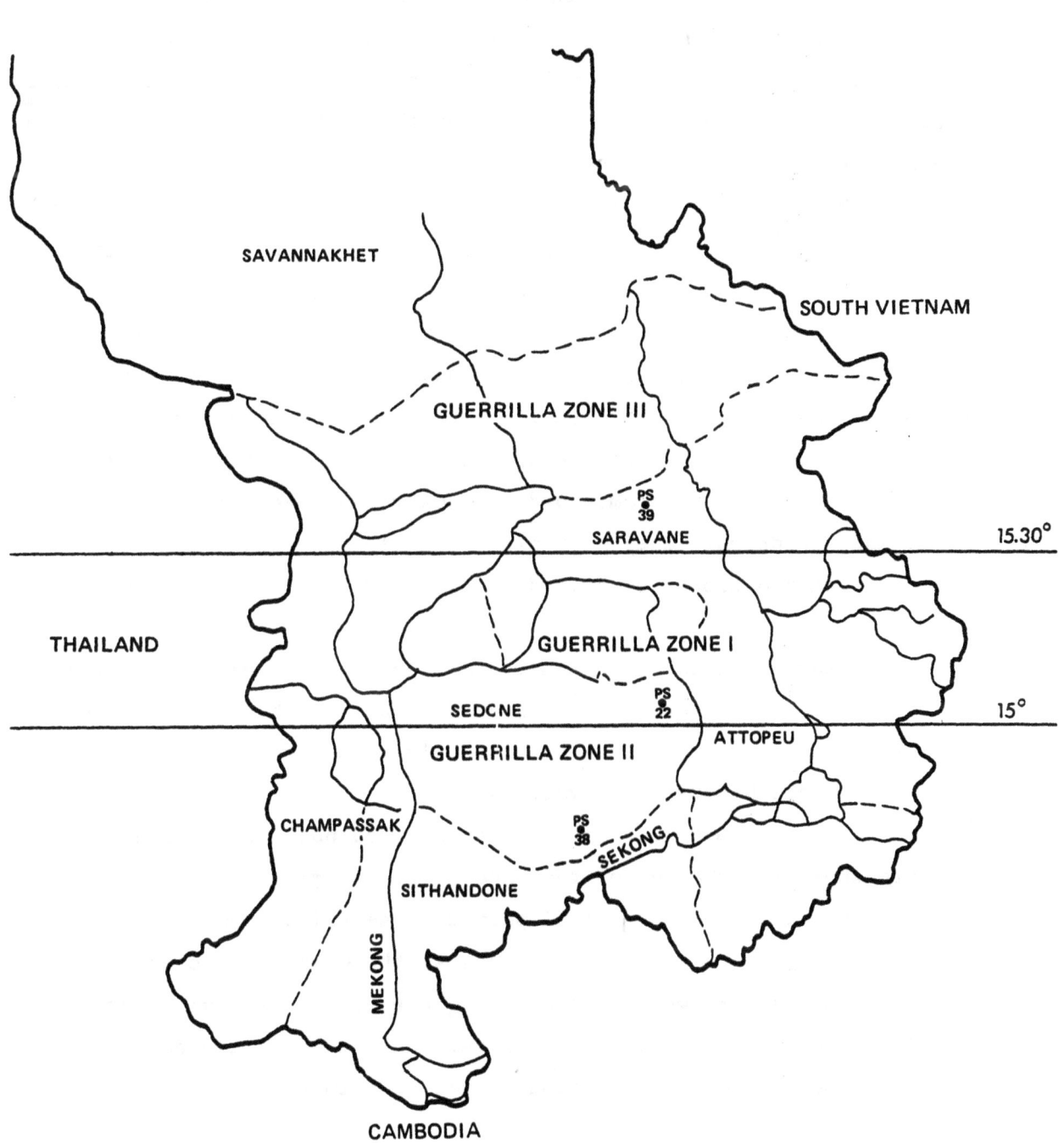

Each guerrilla zone unit was confined to its own area and, to avoid accidents, was not permitted to cross the boundary without prior agreement with the zone commander. They could not operate in a sector assigned to the RLA unless they had the approval of the RLA battalion commander. Coordination, however, continued to be the exception, for unless the irregular unit commander foresaw a possibility of conflict with RLA forces in his intended area of operations, no coordination was attempted. Furthermore, the only missions assigned to irregular units were directly related to interdiction of the Ho Chi Minh trail, not to the preservation of security in southern Laos.

The NVA had well organized road security. They used platoons and trained dogs against our road watch teams. The road watch and action teams in Military Region IV were composed of 12 men each. These teams observed truck convoys along the trail and called for air strikes. Since they could not speak English signals were used in their communications with the U. S. Air Force. They also observed enemy depots and parking areas and gained intelligence through tapping NVA telephone lines. The action teams ambushed and destroyed enemy trucks, ammunition, and POL drums. They also planted anti-tank mines along the trail and photographed trucks destroyed by air raids or anti-tank mines and ambushing.

The teams were taken to their operational areas along the trails by helicopter and covered by T-28s or A1Es during the flight. Occasionally they were sent on foot. Local people were often used in road watch or action teams because they were familiar with the area but this had disadvantages because most of these people had not been trained to perform what was expected of them and their reports could not be relied upon. The enemy also used local people as security teams, but they seemed to sympathize more with us because the enemy had so often used them for hard labor, working them along the trail for long hours with little or no reward for their services, while the RLA did not expect so much from them or use coercion to get them to work.

Laos Irregulars After 1970

North Vietnamese Army actions increased significantly in the panhandle following the *coup* in Cambodia in 1970. In order to gain more territory in western Military Region IV, and to expand the utilization and improve the security of the Ho Chi Minh and Sihanouk trails, the enemy conducted offensive operations with formations up to regimental size, attacking regular and irregular forces in the region. With the closure of the Cambodian ports, the Sihanouk trail gained vital importance as the only major route available for support of NVA forces in central and southern South Vietnam.

I realized that the SGU's were not equipped to deal with the powerful NVA regular forces operating in Military Region IV. As chief of staff for irregular forces in the region, and drawing on my experience as a groupement mobile commander, I began reorganizing the irregular forces in 1970. I had observed through the years of fighting in Laos that independent RLA battalions rarely could operate effectively together as components of a larger force under an unfamiliar commander. The soldiers' and officers' loyalties were too exlusively tied to each's own battalion commander. Furthermore, battalion commanders were slow or reluctant to respond to orders other than those of the military region commander. Consequently, the solution seemed to lie in formally constituting groupment mobiles out of separate irregular battalions. This arrangement would mean that the GM commander would have clear, undiluted authority over promotions and assignments within the GM and, resultingly, receive the loyalty and response he needed from the battalions assigned to the GM. The process of reorganization was completed by October 1971 when the first irregular GM was committed against the NVA.

The GM was composed of four guerrilla battalions and one weapons company. *(Chart 2)* The battalion strength was 300 men; 16 officers and 284 enlisted men. *(Chart 3)* Each rifle company had four officers and 93 enlisted men, with three 30-man rifle platoons. In addition to the

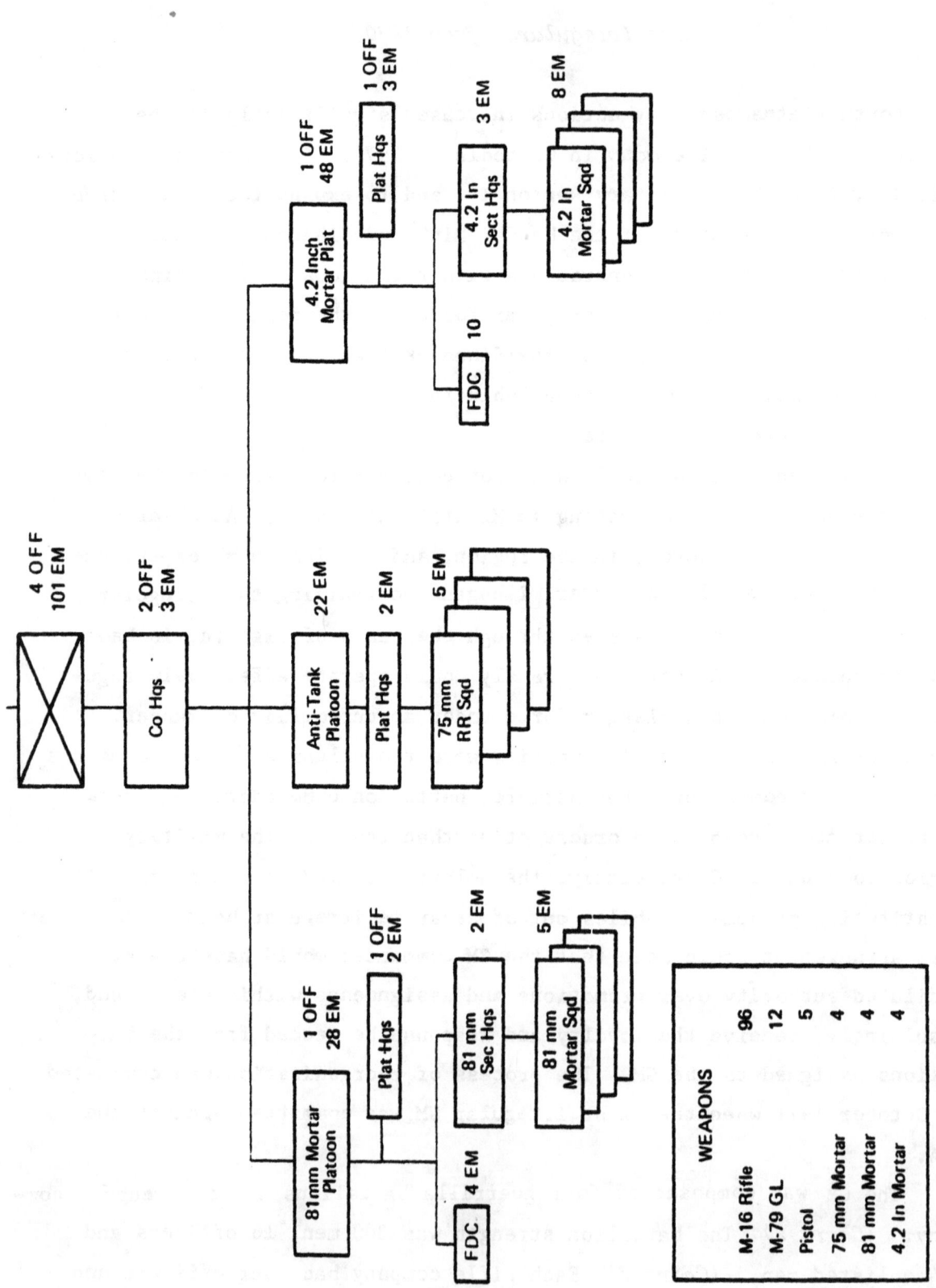

Chart 2 — Lao Irregular Heavy Weapons Company (Organic to GM)

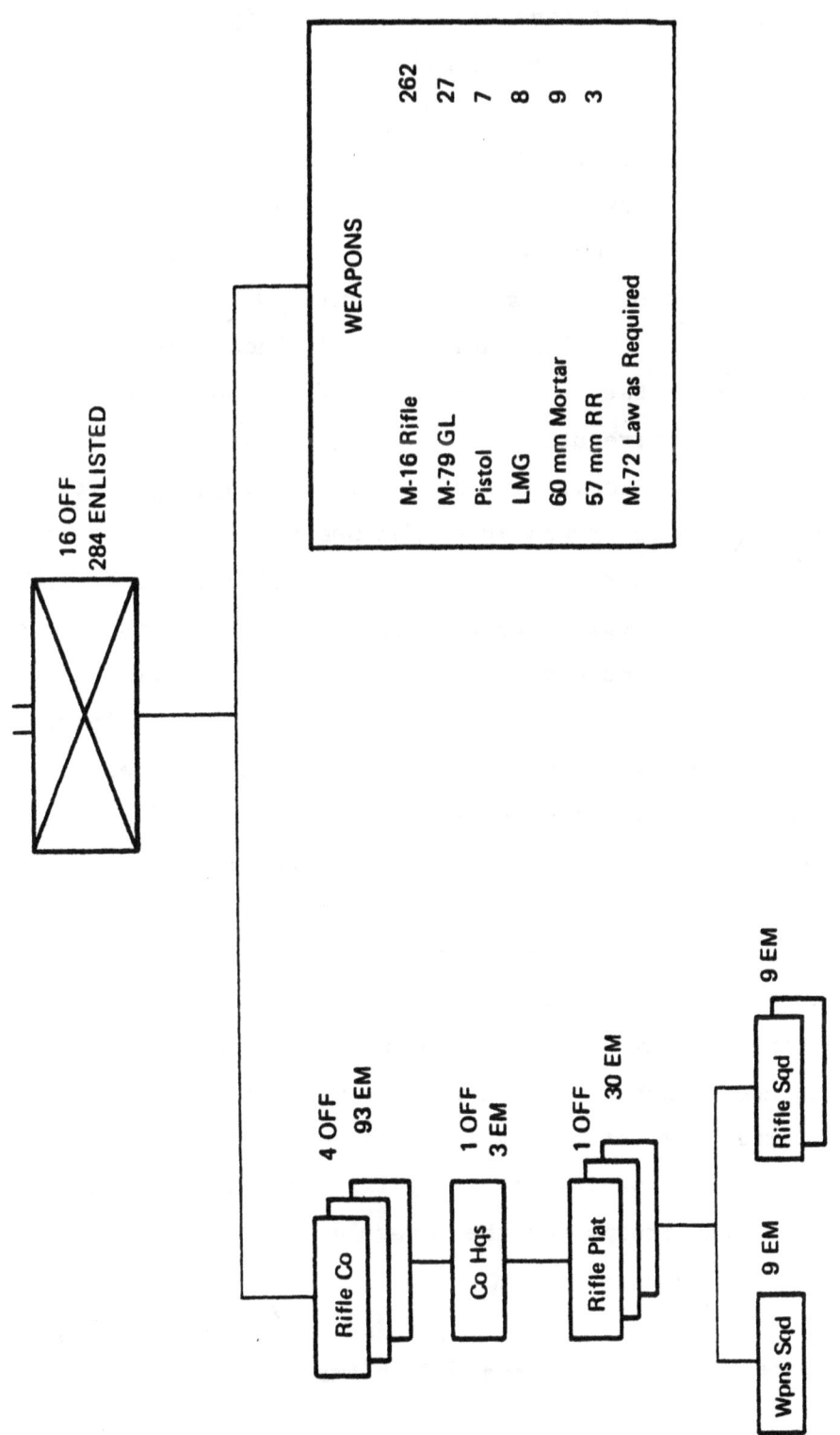

Chart 3 — Lao Irregular Battalion (Organic to GM)

M-16 rifles carried by its riflemen, the battalion had M-79 grenade launchers, M-72 light antitank weapons, eight light machine guns, nine 60-mm mortars, and three 57-mm recoilless rifles.

There were three GM in Military Region IV and one battalion of replacements in reserve at the training camp at PS-18. *(Chart 4)* There were four GM in Military Region III and two battalions of replacements in reserve at the training camp at Savannakhet. *(Chart 5)*

I was appointed MR IV commander in July 1971. With this position came the additional duty of commander of all Laos irregular units in the region. Each of the irregular bases on the Bolovens Plateau was commanded by an irregular colonel and was the base-camp of up to three irregular battalions. All offensive missions against the Ho Chi Minh trail assigned to irregular formations until the cease-fire came from the American leadership which was interested primarily in reducing the flow of men and supplies to Vietnam. These missions were subject to my approval as region commander. The missions originated with the American leadership in Vientiane and were passed to the Americans in Pakse who discussed them with me. I never found it necessary to deny a mission for the irregulars but sometimes, because of military necessity, had to refuse to supply regular support for an irregular mission. It was apparent to me that some of the missions given to my irregulars were not discussed, except in general terms after the action was over, with my superiors in Vientiane.

After the Cambodia *coup* of 1970 and the westward expansion of the Ho Chi Minh and Sihanouk trails, I frequently found it necessary to employ the irregular battalions in a conventional infantry role. The Americans were still paying the irregular troops, but I was responsible for recruiting the troops for the irregular units and delivering them to the irregular bases.

Command Problems

Early in my career as an officer in the Laos Army I became aware of some of the peculiarities of the Laos political and social structure

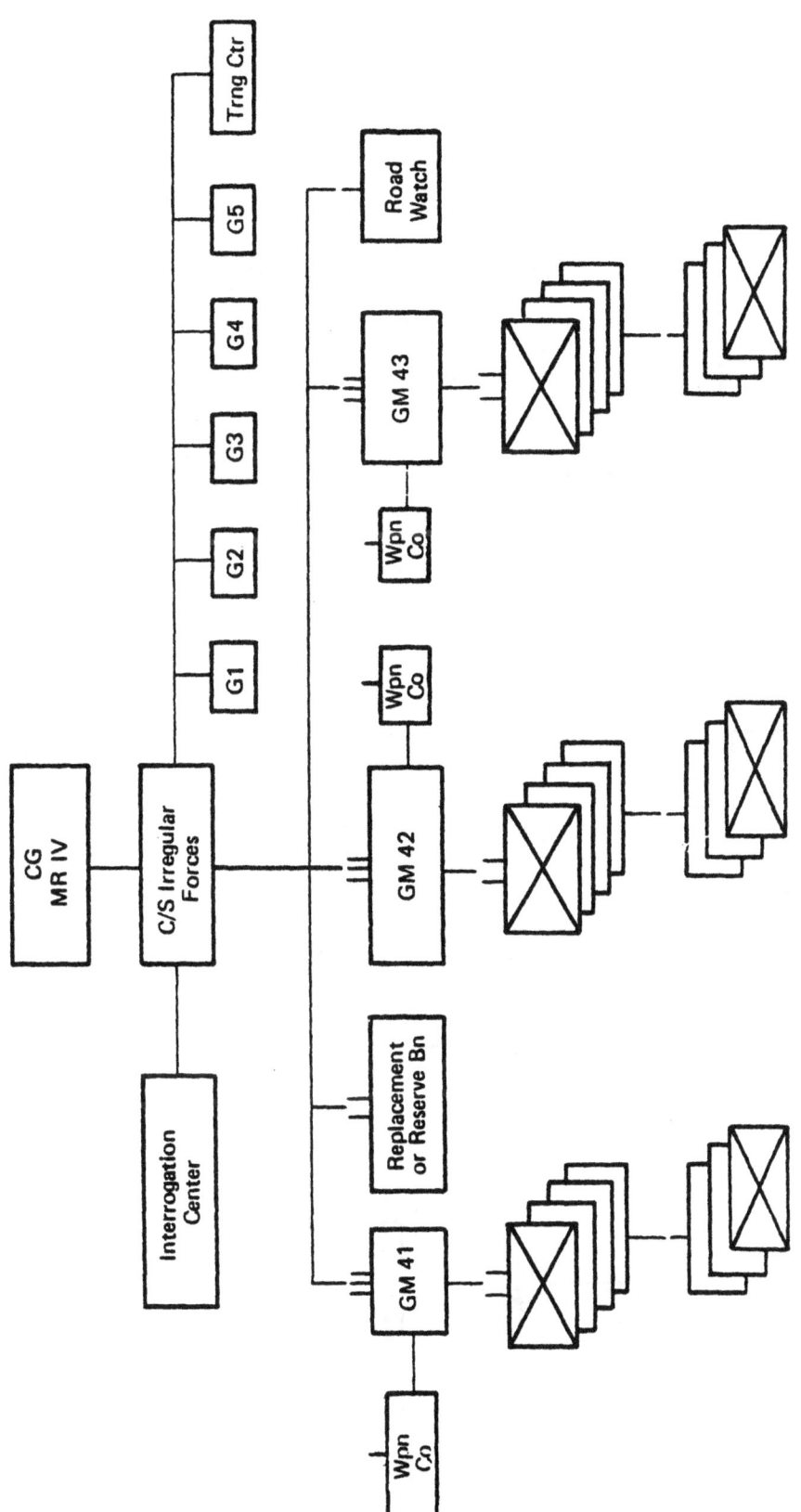

Chart 4 — The Organization Irregular Forces in MR IV After 1970

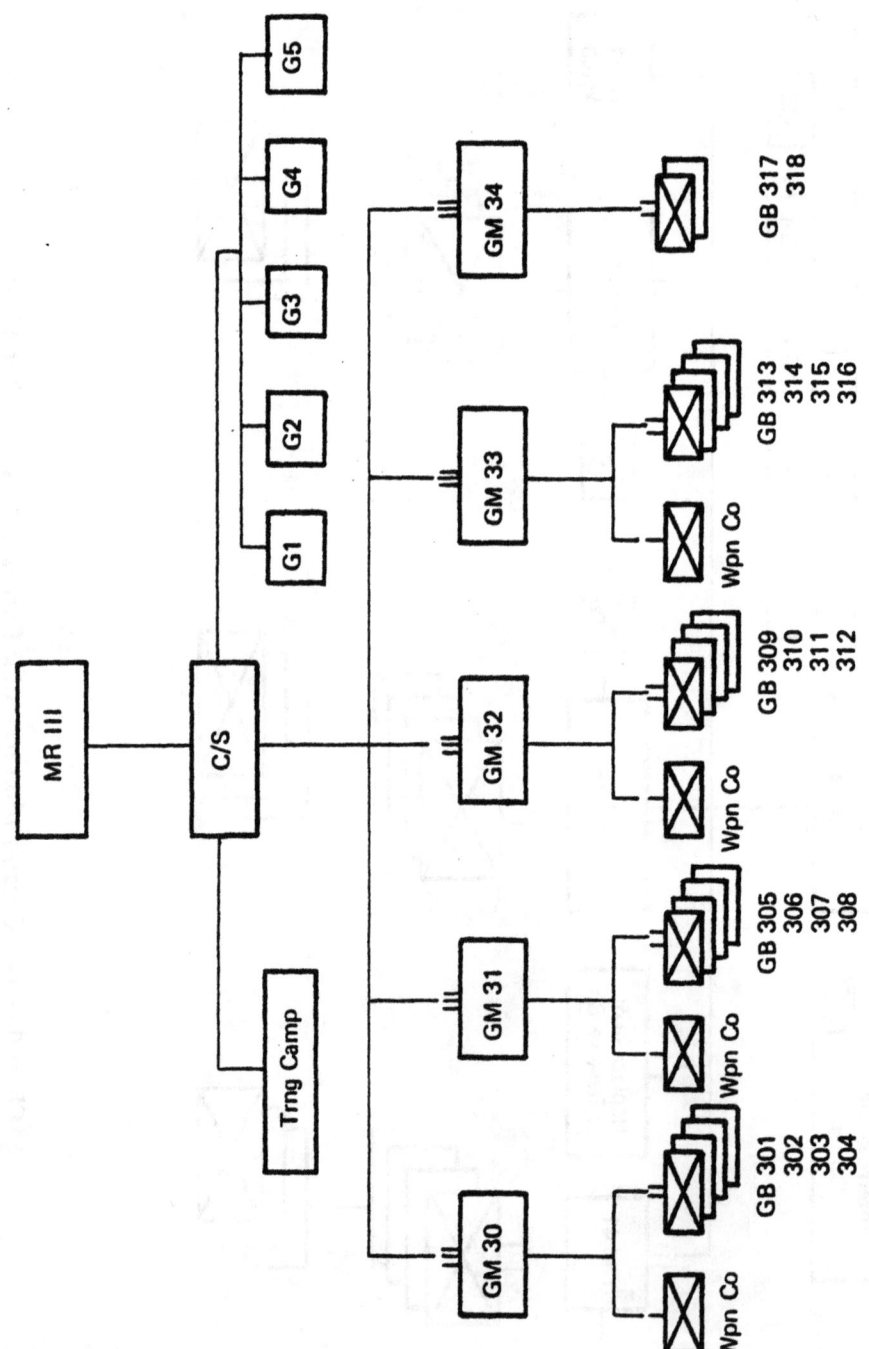

Chart 5 — Organization of Irregular Forces in Military Region III After 1970

that influenced the exercise of command in our army, but it was not until I reached the level of regimental command that these influences became real problems. Then, when I became region commander, these and other command problems occupied a great deal of my time.

Prior to May 1971, the RLA in MR IV was charged with a territorial security mission. This role enabled the 23 battalions of Royalist and Neutralist forces to be employed near population centers where recruiting was relatively easy. Additionally, since there was little chance that these units would be employed in actual combat, their present-for-duty strength was always relatively high. There were also excellent opportunities for the MR IV Commander, General Phasouk, to confer political appointments on relatively poor officers without exposing their ineptness since they were constantly employed in static defensive positions performing routine guard duty and little or no combat, even against the equally inept Pathet Lao forces in their areas. The loyalty of these forces depended largely on who appointed the battalion commander; in almost all cases it was the military region commander. With the exception of the infantry battalion on Khong Island, where the battalion commander was appointed by General Kouprisith, General Phasouk appointed the Royalist battalion commanders and his brother, Colonel Khamsouk, ostensibly the Neutralist commander in MR IV, the Neutralist battalion commanders.[3] With this situation, the regular battalions could not be depended upon for other than the most mundane garrison duties.

Before I became military region commander, the guerrilla force commanders were appointed by General Phasouk also, but in these cases the American advisers had some influence since the troops were paid and supplied by the Americans. Although Phasouk continued to attempt to place his cronies in these lucrative command positions (lucrative because they received pay from the RLG as well as from the Americans, in addition to being in a position to siphon from the top of the troop's

---

[3] General Kouprasith was the most powerful military figure in Vientiane. Not only was he commander of Military Region V, the region in which the capital was located, but he was related to the Sananikone family which, in turn, was the most powerful political family in the capital and among the wealthiest in Laos.

messing funds and combat pay), his attempts were largely negated by the almost daily supervision of the irregular battalion commanders by their American supporters. A battalion commander's weaknesses were soon exposed and relief was quickly forthcoming.

During the period when the irregular forces were charged primarily with operations against the Ho Chi Minh trail structure in the southeast panhandle, the operations were far removed from population centers and the MR IV commander had little knowledge or interest in them. It also is questionable just how much these battalions, operating in 50-man teams, contributed to the war effort. It was a constant hit and run situation with the irregulars doing little hitting and a lot of running. The North Vietnamese were securing the trail structure with regular troops and the 50-man guerrilla teams posed little real threat to them. Still, their presence provided information for the conduct of air strikes and occasionally the troops made a good hit.

Prior to December 1970, the war in MR IV was fought away from Pakse and really meant little to the Lao power structure in MR IV or in Vientiane. Then in December of 1970, the North Vietnamese struck at PS-22 on the eastern edge of the Bolovens Plateau. The NVA raid dispersed the regular battalion, commanded by one of Phasouk's inept brothers, and the irregular battalion which were in the PS-22 garrison. I was ordered to PS-22 to take command of the situation and restore the defense of the shattered camp. Realizing that the RLA troops in the area were scattered and not dependable. I picked up an airborne battalion from Savannakhet -- one commanded by an officer who had commanded a compnay for me in the past -- and took this battalion with me to PS-22. We reoccupied the camp and rounded-up the irregulars who were hiding out in the forest around the camp. I sent Phasouk's battalion of regulars back to Pakse, since it was of no use to me. The NVA attacked again the next morning with artillery, mortars, and recoilless rifles, followed by an infantry assault, but my airborne troops held and we kept PS-22. Although the attack on PS-22 struck some of the Lao in MR IV with the realities of the war, it did not jar them into action.

As alluded to earlier, family power and relationships were real forces to be reckoned with in Laos. These forces, furthermore, were the sources of the most serious problems of command I faced while commander of the MR IV.

Of course, the organization and operation of irregular forces in southern Laos were complex activities because authority was shared by the Americans and the region commander, and this constituted a command problem of some magnitude -- but this problem paled in the light of the difficulties I faced in attempting to execute my command responsibilities in the domain of the large and powerful Nachampassak clan in southern Laos. I succeeded in command General Phasouk S. Rajpheck, a member of the Champassak family, who had been in command for well over ten years. RLA regulations specified a maximum tour of command of three years for this post, but, regulations notwithstanding and in the face of repeated attempts by Americans and influential Lao officials to have him removed, General Phasouk held on. He had two brothers, colonels in the RLA, occupying command positions in the military region -- Colonel Samrane and Colonel Khamsouk -- and another relative, Sisouk Nachampassak, was minister of defense. (While Prince Souvannaphouma was prime minister, he discovered that he could not properly execute his leadership duties and handle the defense portfolio as well, so he asked Sisouk to be defense minister). Each time an effort was made to relieve Phasouk, Prince Boun Oum, the leader of the family, and cousin to the king and the prime minister, would say no.

Finally, however, the pressures became too great, and Sisouk responded to General Oudone Sananikone's request (General Oudone was Chief of Staff) and appointed me the new MR IV commander. As General Oudone told me later, he had argued for a new commander to be chosen not from the south -- for it was certain that any officer from Prince Boun Oum's territory would be Boun Oum's man and just as unresponsive to direction from the general staff as was Phasouk -- but from another region and not under Nachampassak influence. Although I commanded a GM in the south, my home was in the north in Luang Prabang.

Duly appointed, I took command of MR IV on July 1, 1971. My troubles began immediately. First, General Phasouk refused to move from the headquarters. When he finally did, three months later, he returned each weekend and signed orders and directives to a number of the battalions assigned to MR IV. These units were all commanded by relatives of Phasouk and continued to give him their loyalty and to respond to his orders which were generally to avoid any action against the PL or NVA. Examples were BI 20 at Paksong, and later south of Pakse, which belonged to Phasouk's brother Samrane; BI 7, which belonged to Phasouk; and BC 207 which belonged to Phasouk's brother Khamsouk. BV 49 on Khong Island was under the personal influence of General Kouprasith. When I first tried to issue orders to these battalions, the commanders would say that they must first check with Phasouk. The response was usually negative so I learned to do without them until I was eventually able to get some of these commanders replaced. It was not until the end of 1972 that General Phasouk gave up this practice, and I never really gained absolute control over all the units assigned to my command.

The other problem of divided responsibility and command -- that the irregulars responded to orders from Vientiane (and American orders at that) rather than from my Pakse headquarters -- was worrisome and obviously did not enable me to employ my forces to the best advantage for the missions I was assigned. Nevertheless, considering the fact that the irregular mission was Ho Chi Minh trail interdiction and not area defense as mine was, I was able to reconcile myself to this situation without great strain. Furthermore, as the war heated-up in the Bolovens Plateau, the irregulars more and more responded to my direction, and coordination between the Royal Lao Army and the irregular formations improved from necessity.

The final chapter in the brief history of the Lao irregulars was written after the 1973 cease-fire terminated American support and guidance. The Americans were no longer interested in interdicting the Ho Chi Minh and Sihanouk trails, the NVA had greatly multiplied its strength in the panhandle, and the RLG could not assume the support of the irregular battalions. The irregulars were doomed. Eligible officers and soldiers were integrated into the RLA while those not eligible were discharged. This part of the story of the dissolution of the Royal Lao Army is discussed in Chapter V.

CHAPTER III

The Initiation of Conventional Warfare in Southern Laos

Successful operations conducted by RLG guerrilla action teams in the Ho Chi Minh trail area in MR III and MR IV caused increasing concern among the Pathet Lao and NVA forces in South Laos and they responded by creating special units to find and destroy the "team soldiers," as the Lao irregular units were known to the enemy. Increasing the size of our teams was countered by an increase in the size of the enemy units sent out to deal with them; if the irregulars used a section, the enemy used a platoon, etc. A change in tactics was obviously required.

For operations in contested areas, irregular companies were deployed. Twelve-man teams were sent into the Ho Chi Minh trail area to conduct mining, ambushes, and raids on soft targets. Administratively, battalions controlled the operations and administration of the companies. The technique was to have one company operating in the trail area, broken down in teams, one company operating in the contested area at company strength and the remaining company of the battalion in reserve and training status. The "team soldiers" became more experienced in operations, including the use of tactical air, both RLAF and USAF. The enemy responded by attacking our companies in contested areas with PL formations from company up to battalion size. We found that this PL tactic created favorable opportunities to attack the larger enemy units with tactical air strikes and inflict heavy casualties upon them while units were in contact.

Later, as enemy units increased in size and combat power, we found it was better for morale and efficiency to deploy battalions as battalions; that is, a battalion's mission was either team operations under company control, to operate the entire battalion as a battalion in the field, or training and rest for the whole battalion at a time. Experience and hard fighting produced a tough cadre, loyal to individual battalion commanders who proved themselves as capable officers. The influx of NVA units, more heavily armed and supported was also being felt; our tactics had rendered the PL almost ineffective in all of South Laos. It was interesting to note that when a battalion was hit hard and scattered by a superior enemy force, it always reported, "we are now operating as teams."

As late as mid-1970, while I was still C/S, Guerrilla Forces MR IV, NVA battalions usually operated at less than full strength and their armament consisted of light infantry weapons including SKS rifles, AK-47s, sub-machine guns, and 60-mm and 82-mm mortars. Occasionally NVA units would conduct 122-mm rocket attacks against large urban areas. The original mission of NVA units in South Laos was to protect the logistics system moving supplies and men into South Vietnam. As the war in South Vietnam escalated, the NVA high command expanded the system which up to then was confined to the border areas of Laos, South Vietnam and Cambodia. The success of the trail interdiction operations, especially the heavy US air effort, compelled the NVA to disperse and multiply the routes it used through the panhandle. Furthermore, the NVA leadership was well aware of the American reluctance to conduct air strikes close to populated areas in southern Laos. They correctly concluded that if they could shift the logistics system westward into the Mekong and Bolovens region, tucked up against and inside this relatively densely populated area, they could avoid much of the damage being inflicted by US fighter-bombers and B-52s. They, therefore, began moving supplies over roads on the Bolovens Plateau and on the rivers such as the Sekong and the Mekong. To protect this expansion of the logistical effort, the NVA reinforced infantry units in the south in order to confine Laos forces largely to the defense of the cities of Pakse and Savannakhet and prevent them from harassing the line of communications.

Another event had a profound influence on the NVA strategy to shift its logistical network westward in the Laos panhandle. This was the

Cambodian *coup* of 15 March 1970. Before the *coup* Cambodia was technically neutral but steadily leaning to the left. Prince Sihanouk supported the North Vietnamese by letting them use Sihanoukville as a port for receiving their equipment by sea from North Vietnam. The North Vietnamese had no respect for the neutrality of Cambodia and for as long as half of a decade they occupied military sanctuaries all along the Cambodia frontier with South Vietnam; the sanctuaries extended as far as twenty miles into Cambodia. These sanctuaries were used as safe areas from which to launch attacks on the American and South Vietnamese forces and contained major base camps, training sites, hospitals, general logistics, weapons and ammunition depots, air strips (which they used for liaison flights) and prisoners of war compounds.

After the installation of the new government in Cambodia led by Marshal Lon Nol, the NVA and VC in Cambodia were cut off from their supplies through the port of Sihanoukville. Until the change of government in Cambodia, the North Vietnamese supply trail structure running through southeastern Laos into northeastern Cambodia and into South Vietnam was generally confined to the jungled areas. There was little or no population and the area was of no particular strategic importance to the RLG. Only a limited supply flow went into northern Cambodia to support the fledgling Communist movement there. The Sekong River at the eastern base of the Bolovens Plateau through Attopeu provided the North Vietnamese with a natural supply route although up to this time they made but limited use of it.

Despite the full weight of American bombing operations, Ho Chi Minh trail truck traffic increased day by day and the NVA continued to improve the road network, keeping passages open and making roads suitable for high-speed traffic. They also took all steps possible to reduce the effectiveness of US bombing. The bombs made movement along the trail very risky; some of the bombs were fused for delayed action, timed to detonate hours after they were buried in the ground to discourage the road maintenance crews. NVA engineers also improved and expanded the Sihanouk trail and large amounts of rice reached NVA troops fighting in the central highlands of South Vietnam by this route.

To expand and protect the network, the NVA deemed it necessary to eliminate any possible direct threat which could be posed by RLA forces at Attopeu and Saravane. Prior to this time, forces garrisoned at these two major population centers in South Laos had posed no threat to the North Vietnamese because of the ineptness of the RLA and the general "arrangement" between RLA and North Vietnamese forces that neither would bother the other. This relationship between the RLA and the NVA was most prevalent around Saravane and Attopeu and was based upon the commercial dealings of some RLA commanders with the NVA. It amounted essentially to the trading of rice and other commodities needed by the NVA and was carried on through Pathet Lao agents. It began while Phasouk was commanding at Attopeu and continued after he became commanding general of the military region. Because of the profits that accrued to Phasouk and his commanders, no serious efforts could be mounted against this illegal traffic. The NVA eventually put a stop to it when it no longer suited its purposes; that time arrived when Lon Nol deposed Sihanouk. The small NVA operations in the western panhandle would be expanded and these operations would require more terrain, more security and more reliable logistics. The first objective that would be seized to further the NVA objectives would be Attopeu.

Attopeu

Attopeu, situated just below the southeastern escarpment of the lofty Plateau de Bolovens, was the province capital but it had been an isolated enclave since 1962. *(Map 10)* Although it was clearly in view of the RLA positions on the rim of the Plateau, all supply and evacuation of the town had to be by air. The NVA secured Muong May, just across the Sekong River from Attopeu and controlled all land access to the province. Not only were the Sekong and its tributary, the Sekaman which joined it at Attopeu, important elements in the Ho Chi Minh trail system, but National Route 16 led eastward toward the South Vietnam border and joined other parts of the trail system into South Vietnam near Dakto in Kontum Province. In fact, it was less than 50 miles from Attopeu to

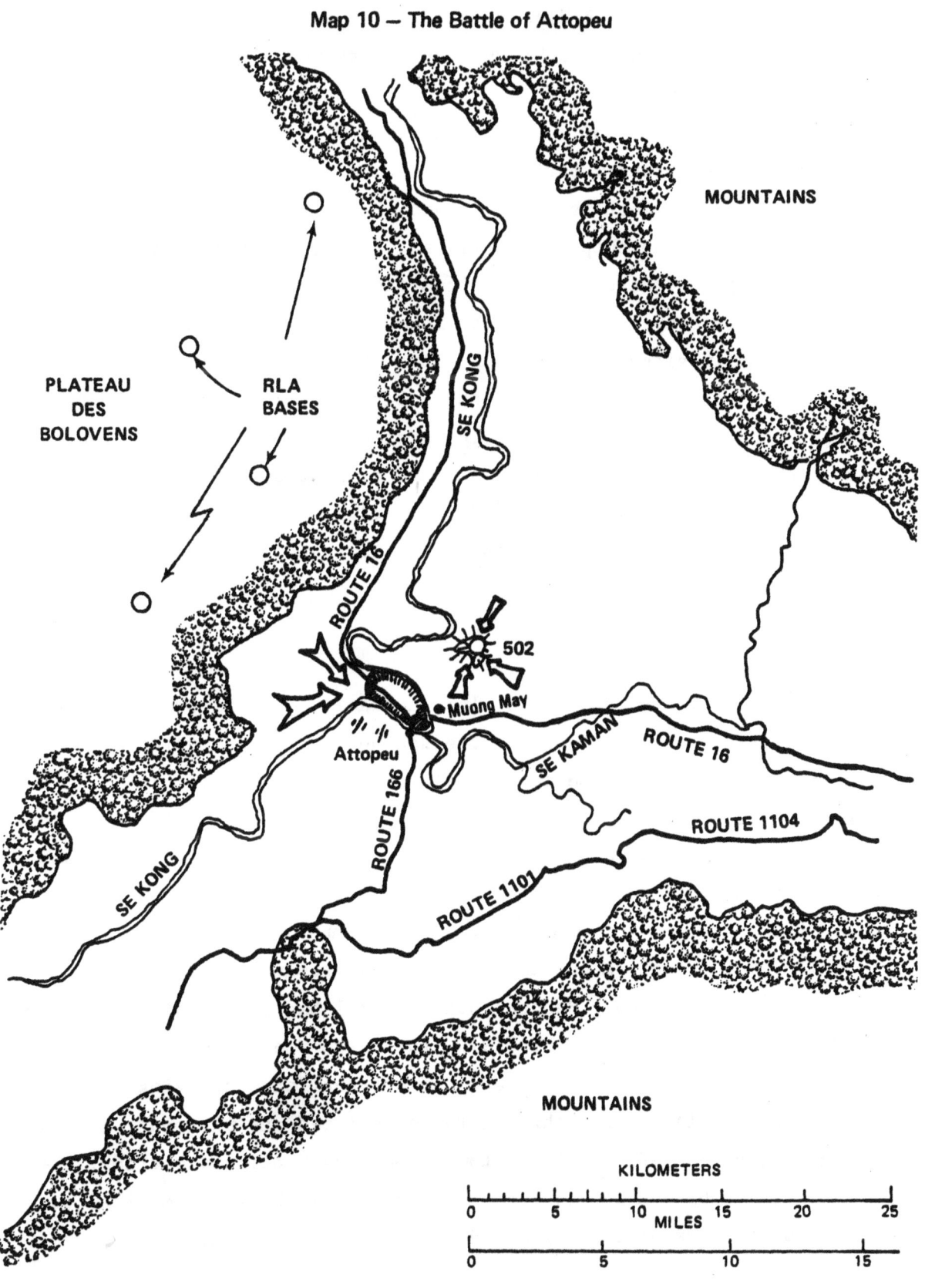
Map 10 — The Battle of Attopeu

Dakto. Attopeu thus became a key feature in the NVA logistics system supporting forces in Cambodia as well as in South Vietnam.

The RLA maintained two battalions in Attopeu, one of which outposted Hill 502 northeast of the town. Infantry Battalion 4 of the old, dissolved Groupement Mobile was there along with Bataillon Volontaire 43 when two NVA infantry battalions launched the attack in April 1970. Supported by 82-mm mortars and 107- and 122-mm rocket artillery, the NVA infantry hit the outpost on Hill 502 first, but the main attack surprised the defenders by coming from the west, closing off the narrow peninsula formed by the bend in the Sekong. With their mortars and rockets ideally sited on the south flank of the RLG positions, the NVA infantry swiftly overran the defense. Dispersed and leaving about 150 of their comrades dead on the field, scattered remnants of the two RLG battalions escaped through the NVA lines or across the Sekong, some to be later caught, along with many fleeing civilians, in well-laid ambushes. Attopeu belonged to the NVA. Saravane was next.

Saravane

Like Attopeu, Saravane was also the capital of its province and it too was a river town situated on the Sedone River and astride a major section of the Ho Chi Minh trail system. About 50 miles north of Attopeu, Saravane was at the junction of National Route 23, which led north to the vital Tchepone area, Route 16 which ran west to Khong Sedone, and other lateral roads and trails that joined other parts of the Ho Chi Minh trail east toward the A Shau Valley of South Vietnam.

The administrative capital of Saravane Province had been removed to the security of Khong Sedone, but it still had a population of up to 20,000 people. Until early 1970, the North Vietnamese were content to bypass Saravane on the east and did not challenge the single RLG battalion (BV 41) and its three attached armored-car platoons which was charged with the defense of the town. But, as mentioned earlier, the weight of the US bombing effort on the Ho Chi Minh trail impelled the NVA to shift some of the logistical operations westward, seeking the passive protection provided by the proximity of the population centers located there.

In May 1970, one month following the seizure of Attopeu, two regular NVA battalions attacked Saravane. The rifle companies of BV 41 which were deployed on outposts and blocking positions as far as 20 kilometers from the town, were not even in position to take part in the battle. The two battalions of NVA infantry concentrated and quickly disposed of the RLA battalion headquarters in Saravane while the companies of BV 41 individually withdrew to Khong Sedone.

Military Region IV gathered some forces — Parachute Battalion 104, BI-4 (reorganized after its withdrawal from Attopeu) and BV 41 — and two days later launched a counterattack. The NVA had strong defenses prepared by this time, supported by artillery and mortars, and the attack failed.

Prior to this time, the RLA had seen little or no combat. The irregulars were organized into 50-man teams for the purpose of conducting raids and ambushes along the Ho Chi Minh trail. In this combat organization they posed no threat to regular NVA units. Further weakening the RLG position in MR IV at this time, two irregular battalions were deployed to MR II to help salvage a rapidly deteriorating situation there. These two battalions gave good accounts of themselves and became the foundation of what was to be a well-organized, conventional, light infantry force under the "irregular" guise in MR IV.

Despite the NVA seizure of Attopeu and Saravane, senior RLA commanders in MR IV tended to disregard the threat. They regarded the attacks against Saravane, Attopeu and the eastern Bolovens for what they were: an expansion of the NVA trail network, and they recognized that there was little that they could do about it with the small, poorly led and inexperienced RLA units. The general attitude was that this was a problem between the South Vietnamese, Americans and North Vietnamese. As a result of this attitude, RLA forces suffered little in the attacks, giving up ground in great chunks in exchange for relatively light casualties.

In 1970, the NVA 9th Infantry Regiment, which had fought against the US Marines in Hue, South Vietnam during 1968, was sent to Laos to prepare to capture the irregular operating bases on the Pleateau de Bolovens. From mid-1970 the NVA continued to reinforce in southern Laos until the 968th Group became a division-sized unit consisting of the 9th, 19th and 29th Infantry Regiments, supported by tanks and artillery. An independent infantry regiment, the 39th, also was organized to operate in South Laos. The 559th Transportation Group retained command of the logistics system.

By February 1971, the North Vietnamese had expanded their holdings in southern Laos considerably. While this provided a buffer for the trail structure, it also provided a large land mass for which it was necessary to provide security. They had large numbers of engineer troops, coolies and security forces along the trail rapidly expanding it for the coming dry season supply offensive which was to be launched when the rains abated in the fall of 1971. They had already completed a significant portion of the supply network. While this system was primarily designed to provide for a rapid flow of supplies, it was to play a significant role in the North Vietnamese containment of the South Vietnamese thrust into southern Laos during Lam Son 719 by providing rapid lateral as well as north-south avenues of approach for NVA.

Tchepone

In February 1971, the South Vietnamese Army (ARVN), with heavy US air support, invaded Laos in the region of Tchepone and the Ho Chi Minh trail in Operation Lam Son 719. This invasion provided a dramatic object lesson illustrating three important points about the trail.

First, the fact that an attempt at ground interdiction was made at all reflects the difficulty of impeding the flow of men and supplies down the trail by air action alone.

Second, the stiff resistance with which the NVA met the invasion was an indication of the large value they attached to this supply line.

In Lam Son 719, South Vietnamese soldiers ran a captured NVA amphibious tank. This Soviet-built light tank mounted a 76-mm gun

Third, the fact that the incursion, which reached as far west as Tchepone, did not significantly reduce the volume of supplies that the NVA was eventually able to move down the trail although the deliveries were no doubt delayed. The NVA's ability to cope with this problem was evidence of the effectiveness of the diffuse system of jungle paths and alternate roads.

Lam Son 719, to the great surprise of senior RLA commanders in MR IV, began with the South Vietnamese, supported by US air, quickly thrusting into southern Laos. It later developed that the RLA commanders in MR IV were about the only ones surprised by Lam Son 719; the foreign press had alluded to it on several occasions and SVN preparations must have been apparent to the North Vietnamese in advance since they were able to move units from North Vietnam to reinforce in the area west of the DMZ. The most significant thing about Lam Son 719, as far as the Lao were concerned, was that it confirmed their belief that the North Vietnamese trail structure was an American/South Vietnamese/North Vietnamese problem and that the principals involved did not regard the RLG position as germane to the issue. This attitude was unfortunate since it was possible that the Lao forces could have played a significant role in Lam Son 719. In retrospect, a RLA thrust, weak as it may have been, along Route 9 toward Chavane from MR III and a RLA threat to Saravane in MR IV may have succeeded in diverting sufficient North Vietnamese forces to have permitted South Vietnamese more success during Lam Son 719.

While Lam Son 719 was in progress, military activity in southern Laos tapered off, MR IV forces should have been regrouping, but this was not to be so; the respite offered by Lam Son 719 was not exploited as senior Lao officials in MR IV continued to view the trail problem as one of the North

Vietnamese versus the South Vietnamese and the Americans. The Lam Son 719 respite was interpreted, incorrectly, as a sign that the North Vietnamese had all they wanted in south Laos, and what the south Laos commanders were content to let them keep was relatively insignificant. They were still far from Pakse, the only key Lao city in MR IV. This interpretation was partially caused by a lack of knowledge of the objectives and up-to-date information on Lam Son 719 developments. The standard joke in MR IV was that the Lao received most of their information on the progress on Lam Son 719 from intercept of North Vietnamese communications while their "allies," the South Vietnamese and the Americans, kept their developments secret.

It is unfortunate that a senior, qualified US Army officer was not present in Vientiane to push for more involvement by the RLA. During this time, the Lao themselves were more concerned with developments in MR II and the threats to life in Vientiane than with the more strategic (in terms of the overall war in Indochina) activities in southern Laos. This was to be the case throughout the Laos war, with the southern Lao feeling like country cousins to the Lao elite in Vientiane who saw the threat in MR II as more directly affecting them. Maintaining the seat of government in Vientiane was undoubtedly a key objective of both the Lao Government and the US Government, however, in light of strategic developments, south Laos was crucial in both the survival of Cambodia and South Vietnam, a fact not fully recognized and accepted by the Lao government or by their American counterparts in Vientiane, much to the frustration of some of the southern Lao leadership.

Following the withdrawal of the ARVN in Lam Son 719, the NVA redoubled its efforts to expand and improve the trail structure. Lam Son 719 was a convincing lesson to the North Vietnamese leadership that this was the correct course of action. Further, the increasing Communist role in Cambodia was requiring larger quantities of supplies which could only be funneled through southern Laos. Recognizing the key role of south Laos, the North Vietnamese upgraded their combat units. The 968th Front became a division and the 9th, 19th and 29th Infantry Regiments were assigned to it with the objective of securing the entire Bolovens Plateau and pushing as far west as Khong Sedone.

While Lam Son 719 may have interrupted the Communist supply flow temporarily, it strengthened the North Vietnamese resolve to further expand in southern Laos and remove any possible threat to a constant flow of supplies. This resulted in significant losses to the RLG when the province capital of Khong Sedone and the key Bolovens Plateau town of Paksong were overrun by the North Vietnamese.

Although Lam Son 719 partially accomplished its objective by temporarily drying up the flow of supplies to the NVA forces in southern South Vietnam and Cambodia, it must be viewed with some doubt by the Lao, for shortly following Lam Son 719, the North Vietnamese significantly upgraded their combat capability in southern Laos, reverting to conventional warfare utilizing regular NVA combat units in regimental attacks supported by long range (122-mm and 130-mm field gun) artillery and, for the first time, armor units in attacks against Lao population centers near the Thai border (Khong Sedone). While it is not certain that Lam Son 719 caused the North Vietnamese leadership to decide on this strategy it certainly must have reinforced their favorable consideration of this course of action. Viewed purely from the stand point of the immediate security interests of the RLG, there were no benefits to Laos from Lam Son 719.

The year 1970 was thus the turning point in the nature of war in the Laos panhandle. Concurrent with the greatly increased demands placed on its logistical and replacement system by the expanded and intensified conventional combat in South Vietnam, the NVA faced serious threats to the continued operation of the Ho Chi Minh trail complex in the panhandle. And not only was the trail under constant attack by American air power, but access to South Vietnam by sea — that is, across the beaches of South Vietnam and through the Cambodian posts — was being denied by US-Vietnamese "Market Time" operations and by the new Cambodian government of Lon Nol. Consequently, to avoid as much US air interdiction as possible, to increase the number of available routes and storage areas in the panhandle, and to develop a greater capability to move supplies through Cambodia, the NVA pushed westward in the panhandle, seizing Attopeu and Saravane in the process. Then, in early 1971, the South Vietnamese attack at Tchepone gave even more urgent impetus to the NVA westward expansion. Conventional combat had come to the panhandle.

CHAPTER IV

The NVA Panhandle Offensives of 1971 and 1972

The ebb and flow of intense NVA activity along the Ho Chi Minh trail generally followed the pattern of the annual wet and dry monsoons that influenced the weather, and hence the trafficability of the roads and trails in the panhandle. As the dry monsoonal winds from China drove the moisture-laden clouds into the Gulf of Thailand, the tropical sun parched the landscape and the laterite roads became hard as concrete, although the dust churned up by the convoys could be seen for miles. It was during these relatively arid months that the NVA usually conducted its Laos offensives, only to withdraw eastward with the coming of the summer rains. But by 1970, this routine pattern was modified; various requirements and pressures combined to compel the NVA to attempt to make permanent its lodgements in the western panhandle.

As recounted earlier, Attopeu and Saravane fell to the NVA in early 1970. The RLA lacked the combat power to even attempt the recapture of Attopeu and the weak counterattack mounted against Saravane had failed. The Saravane population resisted NVA efforts to keep it in the town — the NVA wanted the people around as insurance against air attacks — and had fled. The NVA could not prevent the people from returning to their homes for load after load of their belongings which they carted and carried the 30 miles down Route 16 to Khong Sedone. The people even removed the corrugated metal roofing from their houses. Observing the weakness of NVA security in the abandoned town, Laos Military Region IV and Vientiane authorities began planning an operation to retake Saravane in the next dry season which would begin in late October and last into April.

Irregular Groupement Mobile 32 from Military Region III was selected for the task. Airlift would be provided by the USAF helicopters (CH-53s) from Nakhon Phanom, Thailand. GM 32 was landed on the Saravane airstrip in March 1971 without any NVA resistance. The NVA battalion was completely surprised and had to withdraw. GM 32 mopped-up around Saravane for three weeks before turning over the security mission to BV-41, the battalion that had been driven out by the NVA in 1970.

BV-41 didn't stay long in Saravane. The 39th NVA Regiment moved back to Saravane in April as the 1971 NVA offensive began and BV-41 had to pull back again to Khong Sedone.

In April 1971, the North Vietnamese began to push into the Bolovens Plateau. Although there were no major engagements, the Lao irregulars on the eastern Bolovens were slowly but surely being restricted in the areas where they could move without engaging the NVA forces. By the first of May, they were within the generally accepted zone of security of the village of Houei Kong, a long-time center for irregular forces activity as well as the center of the Montagnard population in MR IV. Although these Montagnard local forces had a good reputation, they were largely untested in combat. The leader, a Montagnard lieutenant appointed by General Phasouk, enjoyed close relations with the Americans as well as with Phasouk and had promised that "no Communist can enter and live" in his zone of responsibility. On 4 May, at approximately 0900 hours, the NVA began to probe the defense of Houei Kong and by 1100 hours, the village was completely abandoned by the RLA and Montagnard irregular forces. Only about 15 of the Montagnard forces withdrew with the lieutenant and the remainder surrendered immediately to the NVA and began assisting in rounding up the remaining irregular resistance. The entire Houei Kong complex fell without ever being assaulted.

At this time the MR IV commander, General Phasouk, was in the hospital for treatment of injuries received in an automobile accident and a totally inept officer, Brigadier General Kane, was in command. He concurred in the abandonment of Houei Kong without even making an effort to support the forces with air strikes and without advising the

Americans that it was even under attack until the withdrawal took place. A desultory effort to get the troops to go back into the defensive positions was unsuccessful; thus, the fall of the Bolovens Plateau began without a battle.

Paksong and Route 23

On 15 May 1971, the NVA attacked Infantry Battalion 20 at Paksong, in the heart of the Bolovens. The attack began at approximately 0500 hours with a mortar and artillery bombardment followed by infantry attacks, supported by armor. By 0700 hours, the battalion had dispersed and Paksong was lost. Scattered pockets of resistance remained for several hours but efforts to reinforce were only half-hearted and unsuccessful. At the time of the attack, BI 20 was commanded by Phasouk's other brother, Colonel Samrane. He was most famous for his ability to control the coffee and vegetable exports from Paksong and for his conduct of a profitable business with the Pathet Lao, supplying them with rice, gasoline and other needed supplies in return for coffee.

With the fall of Paksong, the real threat to Pakse was finally understood by the MR IV hierarchy as well as in Vientiane. Phasouk called upon General Khong, one of his subordinate generals, who had no specific duty at the time but who had formerly commanded guerrilla units, and told him to organize a task force to retake Paksong. General Khong established a command post and gathered some battalions but delayed making any move toward Paksong until the Vientiane headquarters, prodded by the Americans, lost patience with the inactivity and directed me to regain Paksong. I was given command of a task force consisting of three battalions, BV 41, BV 44 and one Neutralist battalion, BP 104.

The first advance toward Paksong failed when one of my battalion commanders, Lt. Colonel Bouathong, was killed by a short round of artillery and his battalion fell back in disarray. When the NVA discovered this, its forces moved another 10 kilometers west toward Pakse. I moved forward to take personal control of the disintegrating command and deployed two battalions by helicopter to meet the advancing NVA west of Paksong. This element of the task force was too light to stop the NVA

Troops of BV 44 Assemble in the Saravane Area

but it did slow the enemy advance and gave me a chance to reorganize the shattered formations along Route 23 and did buy some time for other Lao forces being assembled elsewhere in MR IV.

My command fought a delaying action and established defensive positions near kilometer 28 on Route 23, 28 kilometers east of Pakse. This was the only real defensible position between Pakse and Paksong and was a bloody battleground for the remainder of the war. So many Laos and North Vietnamese were killed in this area that it became a "haunted place" to the Lao.

On the morning of 11 June, the positions were overrun and the Lao, broken into small groups, were evading to the west. Lao casualties were over 100 killed, an unknown number wounded and several hundred missing. The group with me knocked out a North Vietnamese PT-76. Clearly visible from the air, it provided the first concrete proof that North Vietnamese armor was indeed being employed in MR IV. Additionally, North Vietnamese units in columns of twos could be plainly seen on both sides of Route 23 moving westward. Aerial observers directed sortie after sortie directly onto the North Vietnamese closely bunched together and their casualties were high. The eight RLAF aircraft assigned to Pakse flew 88 sorties on 11 June, a record high for that small number of aircraft. Additionally, the U. S. Air Force joined in the attack of the NVA column. These air strikes can be credited with stopping the NVA and inflicted sufficient casualties to force the North Vietnamese to regroup; it was several weeks before they were in condition to continue their efforts against allied defensive positions along Route 23.

The Lao military structure in MR IV was almost totally destroyed in the series of battles between Paksong and kilometer 23. Seven RLA infantry battalions, two Neutralist battalions, and almost all of the irregular forces were so shattered that they had to be considered combat ineffective. It was then that the reorganization of the military structure in MR IV began. It is impossible to imagine more trying circumstances under which to begin attempting to rebuild the MR IV forces. Concurrent with the poor state of combat effectiveness there was great concern about the NVA capability and intentions to continue the attack toward Pakse.

On 1 July 1971 I became commander of MR IV and immediately began working on a plan to recapture Paksong. Because our reorganization was still incomplete in the region, Vientiane agreed to let us employ GM-32 from MR III. It was to be an airmobile operation with a ground link-up and the airlift would be provided by the USAF CH-53s from Nakhon Phanom. On 15 September, GM-32 poured from its USAF helicopters east of the Paksong road junction and seized the high ground north of the town. Meanwhile, BI-7 landed southeast of Paksong and attacked to seize the high ground south of the town. *(Map 11)* The airmobile assault completely surprised the 9th NVA Regiment, whose main defenses were along Route 23 west of Paksong, and these positions were being attacked by RLG Neutralist Battalions BP 104 and BC 207.

The NVA bunkers and fighting positions were well fortified, heavily manned, and sited in depth along Route 23 west of Paksong and the advancing Neutralist battalions met strong resistance. But cut-off from the rear by GM-32 and BI-7, and under heavy air and artillery attack, the NVA 9th Regiment had to pull out of its Paksong defenses and to avoid annihilation or capture, break into small groups and withdraw through the forest. In three day's time, we had control of the high ground and Route 23 into Paksong.

The success of this operation can be attributed to the surprise of the airmobile assault and to the aggressive attack of GM 32 in driving into Paksong causing the NVA defenses facing the Neutralist forces to collapse. It bought more time for the reorganization of the irregular forces in MR IV and in this respect, it was totally successful. Although Paksong was recaptured by the NVA after the withdrawal of GM 32, this effort required the North Vietnamese to expend more combat power and by the time the North Vietnamese were in position to again threaten Pakse, the irregular forces in MR IV were as ready as they were ever to become to halt the NVA drive and launch a counteroffensive.

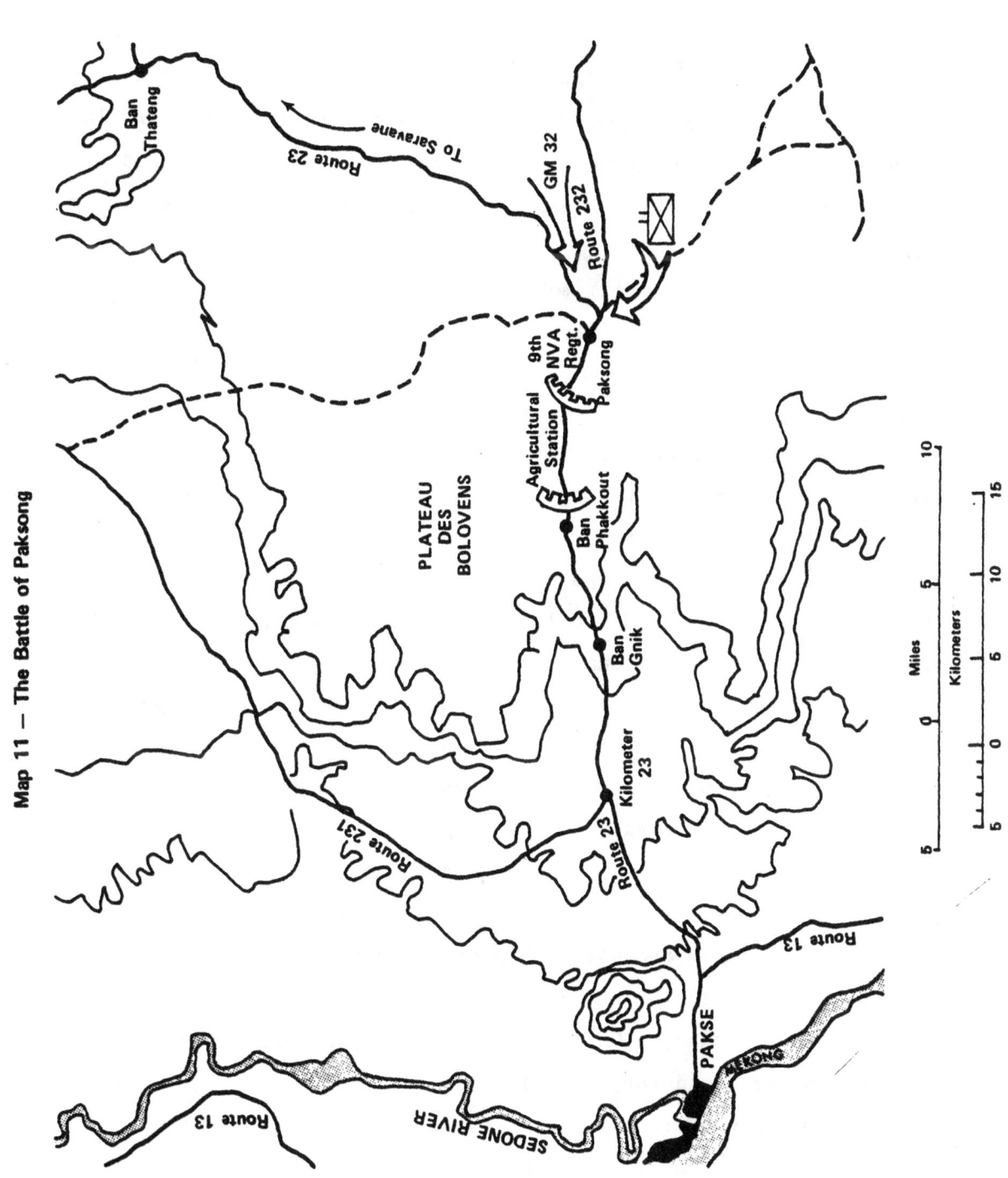

Map 11 — The Battle of Paksong

Reorganization

As mentioned earlier, a complete reorganization of MR IV was underway in the summer of 1971. Where previously the irregular units had been employed in 50-man teams to harass the North Vietnamese, we in MR IV had decided that larger combat formations were needed to provide strike forces to deal with the large formations the NVA was employing with such success. Accordingly, authority had been received for the formation of two groupements mobile consisting of four battalions each with supporting light artillery. We traded ground for time. Fortunately, the NVA casualties in the campaign had been so high that the NVA was unable to exploit its success at Paksong with a strong advance to Pakse.

During the period July-October 1971, the irregular forces reorganization was completed. The first new irregular battalions began arriving at PS-18 in July 1971 for a four month training cycle which included basic individual, basic unit, advanced unit and field maneuvers as well as training in the employment of air and artillery. A major portion of the training was devoted to platoon, company and artillery exercises. Training in large scale airmobile air operations was also given. Although the soldiers after only four months of training were less than outstanding, they were able to hold their own for sustained periods, up to four months. Experience developed following their deployment indicated that after four months of combat, these soldiers had to be pulled from the field or risk total disintegration of the unit. This was amply demonstrated in late 1970 and early 1973 during the period of cease-fire negotiations when the irregulars were left in the field for extended periods. In one case, a GM began to disintegrate after four months but remained in the field for an additional two months. In the other case, the GM also began to fall apart after only 90 days in the field but managed to hold on for five months.

At the same time, a reorganization of the regular and Neutralists forces was also initiated although with considerably less success than with the irregulars. Also it was very difficult to find qualified commanders for the new regular GMs. Although the position was prestigious, none of the many colonels in MR IV wanted the position because of the risk of combat it entailed. Filling the battalion commander positions was even more difficult and eventually many of the younger officers got their chances to lead battalions in combat although they were not, in fact, senior enough to be battalion commanders. Nevertheless, in MR IV we did manage to organize two new regular GMs, 4001 and 4004, with regular and Neutralist battalions.

Complicating the reorganization was an unresponsive support system which never achieved the proficiency of the support system for the irregulars. The essential difference lay in the fact that the irregulars were supported by an American civilian agency, using American helicopters and airplanes, with Americans directly involved in the day-by-day operations of the system. On the other hand all categories of support for the regulars came through the U. S. Military Assistance Program. This support was provided at the national level and entered the RLA system there. The young RLA lacked the experienced logisticians, technicians, and transport to make the system work efficiently. Further complicating the reorganization was the ingrained custom in MR IV that certain battalions belonged to certain senior officers and could not be used without long negotiations with these officers.

The advantage of the irregulars was that they could be used anywhere in MR IV on short notice and that they were commanded by the best officers in MR IV, all volunteers, as were the soldiers in the battalions. Despite the many problems, two training sites were in full swing in the summer of 1971 with PS-18 training irregulars and PS-46 training the regulars.

Concurrent with the reorganization of the regular and irregular forces, a communications and command and control system had to be

developed and installed that could coordinate the many actions in MR IV
in a coherent manner. *(Chart 6)* To accomplish this, a tactical operations center (TOC) was opened with trained tactical air controllers on
duty 24 hours a day. The MR IV staff was reshuffled to provide a streamlined G-2/G-3 section operating side-by-side and the G-1/G-4 section
combined under one support command. The activation of the TOC was to
prove to be the most important staff facility added to the MR IV headquarters.

In establishing the TOC, it was necessary to build a communications
system capable of communicating with all military units in MR IV. To
accomplish this, a relay station was established on a tall mountain
eight kilometers from Pakse. Initially, this station was manually operated with a team of radio operators permanently stationed there. Later,
an automatic relay system was installed on the mountain, greatly facilitating communications. This facility proved invaluable in conducting the
various operations throughout the region as well as enabling the MR IV
staff to coordinate air support requirements day and night. The establishment of this facility alone can be credited with the sustained defense
of Saravane and Paksong just prior to the cease-fire in 1973. Although
it may be difficult to imagine in this day of instant communications,
prior to the establishment of the TOC it was quite possible that an
entire battalion would be overrun before any word of trouble reached MR
IV. In several instances, the word filtered to MR IV headquarters through
the civil communications system several hours later.

Saravane

In September 1971, the NVA 19th Regiment was occupying Saravane.
Our new irregular GM 41 and GM 42 had completed their organization and
training and we saw an opportunity to test them in combat against this
regular NVA infantry regiment. We named our plan to retake Saravane
"Operation Black Lion" and scheduled it to begin in mid-October.

On 16 October, GM 42 air-assaulted from USAF CH-53s west of Saravane
and attacked toward the southeast, clashing immediately with elements of

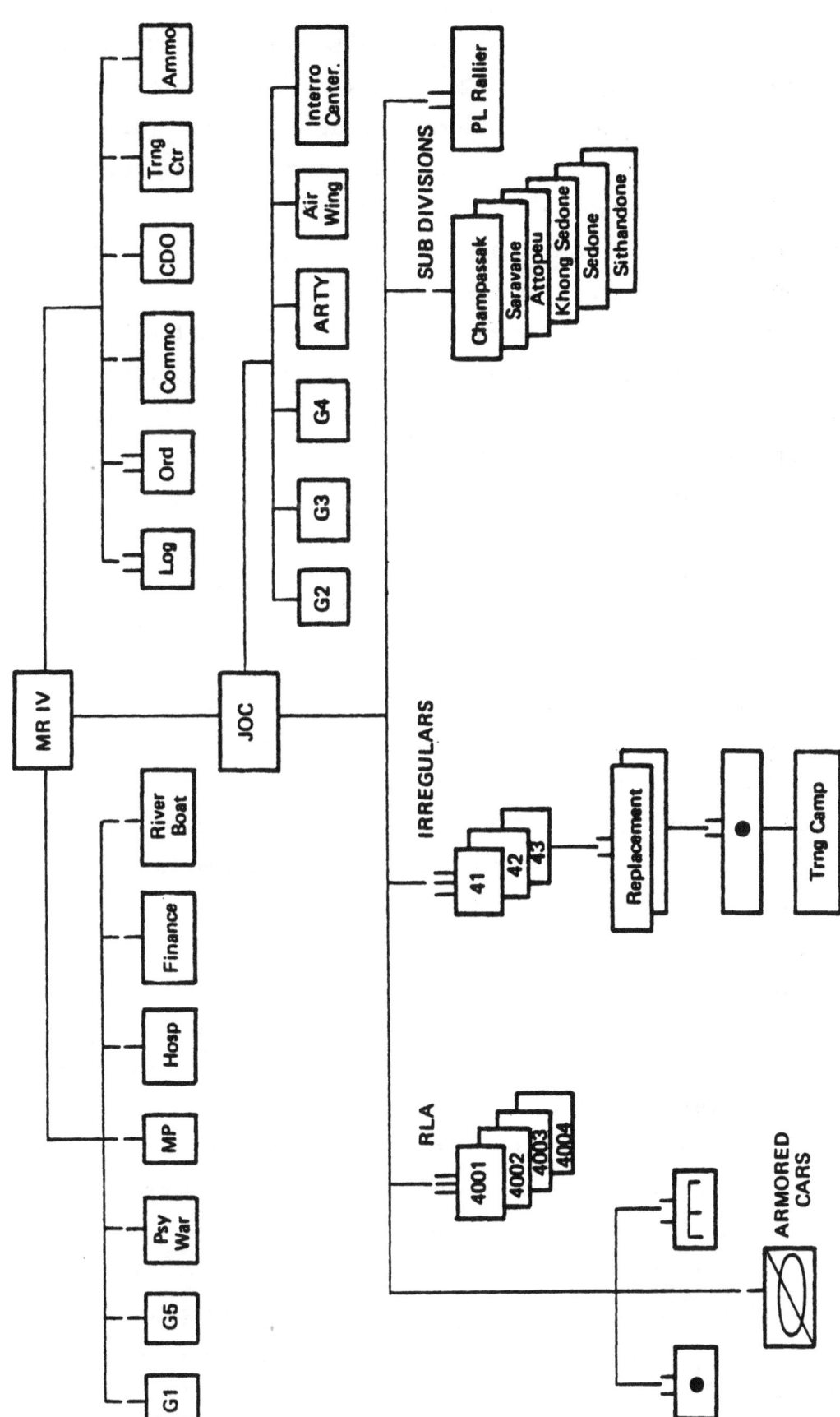

Chart 6 — Organization of Military Region IV in September 1971

the NVA 39th Regiment. Seizing some defensible terrain, the GM dug in and held its ground. Two days later, GM 41 took the NVA completely by surprise by air-assaulting on the northern edge of the town. *(Map 12)* The soldiers of GM 41 and their commander were natives of this province and they knew the terrain very well. They moved quickly into Saravane, eliminating a battalion of NVA troops on the way. Within a week, the two GMs were in complete control of the Saravane area.

Because Saravane was a key junction of the Ho Chi Minh trail, the NVA could not allow this situation to prevail. Using heavy artillery support and dense anti-aircraft fire that denied effective close air support and air resupply, three regiments of NVA regular infantry counterattacked. After more than a month of heavy combat, the two irregular GMs had to be withdrawn, but they had accomplished their mission and had provided more time for the reorganization of forces in MR IV.

During the time GM 41 was at Saravane, the American leadership in Saigon and Vientiane were planning to deal a telling blow to the Communist support structure northeast of the Bolovens Plateau. Intelligence reported the formation of a major North Vietnamese support facility, Binh Tram 37, in the area between Ban Thateng, north of Paksong, and the eastern edge of the Bolovens. The initial objective of GM 41 in Saravane was to buy time for the reorganizations proceeding in MR IV, but this objective was expanded, at the urging of the Americans, who saw an opportunity to find and destroy Binh Tram 37.

An element of GM 41 was air-landed on top of the hill which overlooked Ban Thateng and the valley to the east. One battalion of GM 41 began a drive from Saravane, south toward Ban Thateng. GM 33 was airlifted into the eastern area of the valley and began to drive toward Ban Thateng. In the planning stages of this operation, there was never any intent to hold ground or spend any length of time in the objective area. GM 33 was to air-land, with the elements of GM 41 providing fire support from the fire support base established on top of the mountain, while the other battalion from GM 41 was to serve as a diversion and to provide an escape route for GM 33 and the troops manning the small fire support base. GM 33 was initially very successful, uncovering several trucks, several rice storage areas and ammunition dumps, all of which were destroyed.

Map 12 — The Battle of Saravane

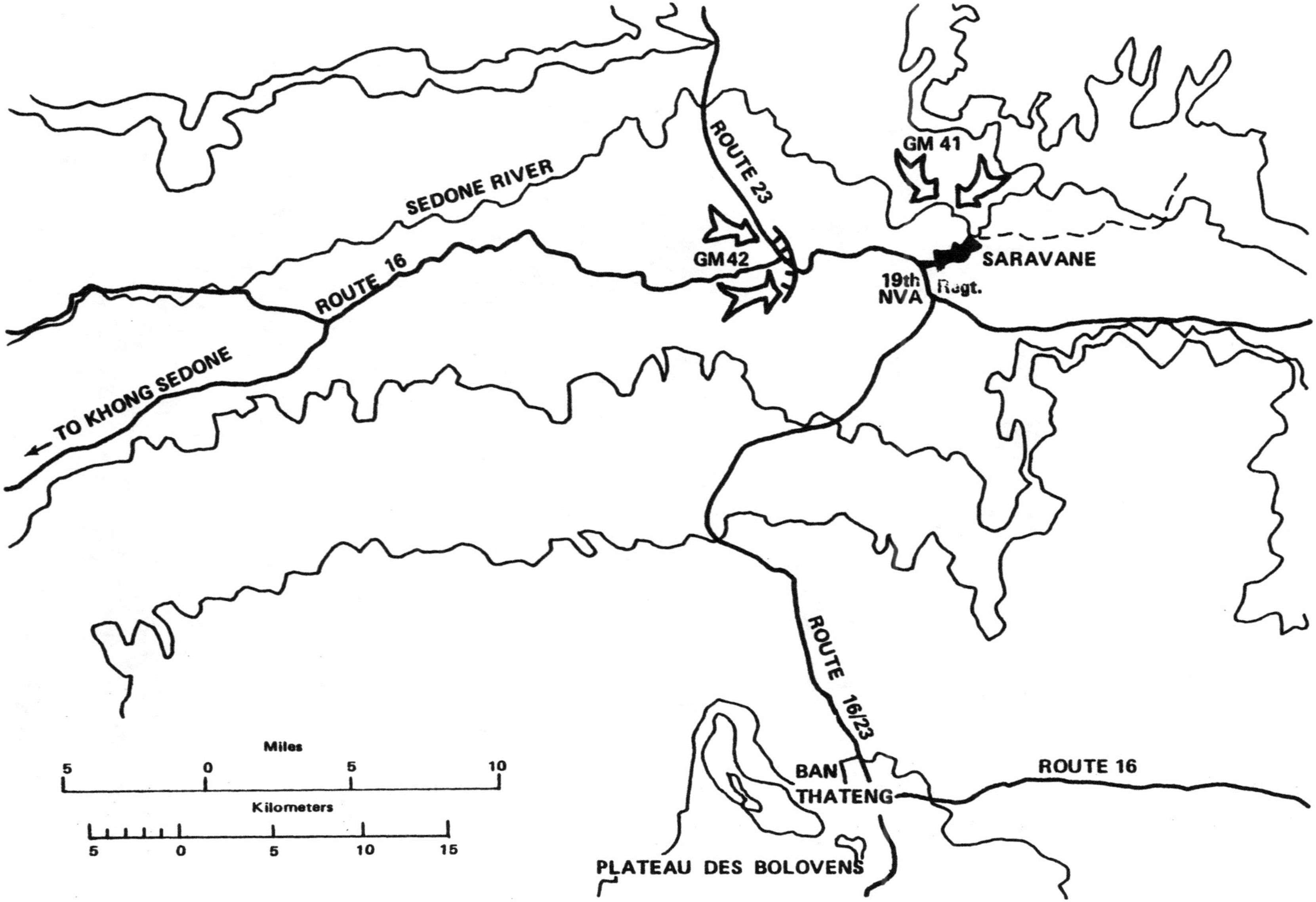

NVA Ammunition Truck Destroyed by Air Attack in Support of the Saravane Operation

The GM continued its rapid movement to the west through the valley with minimum casualties, overlooked on both sides by the North Vietnamese who controlled the high ground. It became obvious that Binh Tram 37 was not in the valley, although it was equally obvious that a branch of this Binh Tram was in process of being established when disrupted by GM 33. Unfortunately, the American fixation on uncovering this Binh Tram and American intelligence insistence that it was there, led to new orders which directed the GM to retrace its steps to the east and begin a systematic search of a large swampy area to the north of the small village of Lao Ngam, off the northeastern edge of the Bolovens. Despite a concentrated search of eight days however, no further trace of the Binh Tram was discovered. Meanwhile, the North Vietnamese began to react to the GM 41 presence near Ban Thateng and exerted considerable pressure. GM 33 escaped through the blocking positions of GM 41 just before the battalion manning the blocking positions was overrun along with the fire base. The major lesson learned from this operation was to never let hopes exceed common sense; in this case, common sense dictated the early extraction of GM 33 according to plan to prevent major losses. The loss of the battalion from GM 41 contributed to the rapidly deteriorating situation at Saravane which may have been forestalled had the battalion at Ban Thateng been able to escape relatively unharmed.

A lesson never really learned was that the Lao irregulars were excellent in rapid raid and destroy missions but were neither armed nor trained to face the major NVA combat formations. With the Lao irregulars, it was better to make your impact as large and as quick as possible then withdraw or delay before the NVA could bring to bear its full combat potential. The rapidity with which the irregulars could be employed versus the rather ponderous, slow-moving combat formations of the NVA was never fully exploited. A GM was committed, did well initially, then was left too long in the false hope that it would be able to stand up to the superior firepower and strength of the NVA. In retrospect, it would probably have been better to trade territory to the NVA for the flexibility which combat-effective irregular GMs provided. With these GMs it was possible to strike anywhere in MR IV, force the NVA to deploy to meet the threat, then withdraw before engaging in decisive combat which the irregulars could never win. This tactic, although much discussed, was never implemented, primarily because of the continuing hope that the GMs would be able to hold the ground they seized so easily. Political considerations, of course, made it hard for the Lao to give up territory without a fight. A recaptured population center (or, more properly, a former population center) became a symbol the Lao political structure in Vientiane could not give up without a struggle. A lesson learned from this is that political and military officials should agree in advance on objectives which could realistically be achieved, then stick to these objectives regardless of temptations. Modifications must be based on facts rather than hopes.

Responding to the capability of the South Vietnamese to interdict the Ho Chi Minh trail in force, demonstrated at Tchepone in February 1971, and to the newly experienced fighting strength of the Lao irregulars, the NVA heavily reinforced in the panhandle during this period. Replacements were infiltrated until all three regiments of the 968th Division were at full strength and reports of heavy artillery, 85-mm, 122-mm and 130-mm field guns, began to filter into MR IV from various road watch teams. Unfortunately, like the reports of enemy armor prior to the attack on Paksong this intelligence was generally disregarded by the Lao leadership in Vientiane and like the reports of the enemy armor, this failure was to prove costly. Vientiane generally disregarded the reports because new heavy artillery would mean "widening the war" and Vientiane clung to the belief that the North Vietnamese still had some respect for the 1962 accords and would not introduce new weapons. The Communists were to prove this assumption totally wrong on numerous occasions.

During this interval, the battle of Paksong shifted back and forth. The Communists recaptured it in December 1971, as related below, when the Neutralist troops withdrew after the two battalions deserted their positions around the two mountains to the west of Paksong. The Neutralists blamed each other for the withdrawal, but the fact is that they withdrew without orders and in the face of almost no pressure. This started another exodus down Route 23 toward Pakse and GM 42 was placed in defensive positions at kilometer 28 with orders to halt the advance. The GM held in the face of repeated Communist assaults and while subjected to heavy mortar and artillery fire. When the GM was finally withdrawn, it had lost over half its original strength and was never again to regain the state of combat effectiveness which it demonstrated in this campaign. Although it performed remarkably well in the capture of Saravane late in 1973, it never recovered from the casualties suffered in the battles at kilometer 28.

Khong Sedone

As mentioned earlier in connection with the ebb and flow of NVA forces at Saravane, Khong Sedone had become the refuge of citizens escaping from Saravane as well as the administrative center for Saravane Province. More important, however, from a strategic point of view, it was on the west bank of the Sedone River, at the junction of National Routes 13 and 16, only 15 miles east of the Thai border and 40 miles north of the region headquarters at Pakse. If the Communists could seize and hold Khong Sedone, they would effectively isolate Military Region IV from the rest of the country. This is exactly what they tried to do; the first time was in January 1972.

Surprised and overwhelmed by the weight of the NVA assault, the RLA garrison at Khong Sedone had withdrawn as the NVA 39th Regiment invaded the town. The Communist were not permitted to remain, however. Borrowing GM 32 from Savannakhet, MR IV counterattacked and recaptured Khong Sedone in February. The defense of Khong Sedone was then turned over to GM 4001 which put one of its battalions, BV 44 in the main defensive position.

In early July, the NVA struck Khong Sedone again. A heavy artillery and rocket bombardment preceded the infantry assault that took BV 44 by surprise at 0530 hours. The battalion was quickly routed by the NVA attack and the Communists gained control of the town. When I learned of the hasty withdrawal of BV 44, I realized that the battalion would have to be reorganized before it could counterattack. I sent it a new battalion commander, relieving the old one who was a hold-over from Phasouk's regime, and ordered it to retake Khong Sedone. Its attempt, poorly supported by only one four-gun battery of 105s, failed. It was obvious that the NVA, with heavier and longer range artillery, were beyond the capability of BV 44. The only other unit I had immediately available was GM 41. It was retraining at PS-18 where it had just been rotated from the delaying actions at Saravane in a very poor state of combat effectiveness. Although we tried an airmobile envelopment in favor of another frontal attack, the GM was also unable to crack the hastily established Communist defenses at Khong Sedone. I eventually had to withdraw it before it was completely destroyed.

The NVA 39th Regiment established some strong defenses at Khong Sedone that were amply supported by artillery. We, at MR IV, knew that the longer we permitted it to remain, the tougher its defenses would become.

With GM 4001 providing route security and protecting the artillery south of Khong Sedone, we again called upon GMs 32 and 33 from MR III to retake the town. On 20 July, GM 32 air-assaulted from USAF CH-53s northeast of Khong Sedone and Ban Nakadao. Meanwhile, GM 33 landed northwest of the town with its four battalions and attacked south, its left boundary (with GM 32) was Route 13 and its objective was the high ground west of Khong Sedone. *(Map 13)*

GM 32 attacked with two battalions generally along Route 13; the other two battalions followed the Sedone River into the town. After a week of heavy fighting, GM 32 forced its way into Khong Sedone, capturing nine soldiers of the NVA 39th Regiment along the way. Its attack was well supported by artillery and air strikes.

GM 33, the right arm of the attack, ran into heavier resistance and had more difficult terrain to traverse. Nevertheless, by mid-August, it too had accomplished its mission. GM 4001, advancing from the south, was also slowed by the enemy resistance as well as by the August rains that made movement on the slippery roads and trails very difficult.

This battle of Khong Sedone destroyed almost half of the NVA 39th Regiment, as well as a good part of the NVA 19th Regiment, including its commander. In its withdrawal, the NVA left behind large quantities of weapons, including one 122-mm howitzer, a 122-mm field-gun, a 75-mm gun and a 37-mm anti-aircraft gun.

An interesting sidelight of this battle was the effort devoted to securing a USAF CH-53 which had been damaged during landing. One battalion from GM 42 was pulled from its training mission to defend the helicopter until it could be extracted by the USAF. Ten days later the helicopter was extracted relatively unharmed, while the battalion had suffered over 100 casualties protecting it; a rather remarkable expenditure of manpower at a time when manpower had become a most critical resource.

Saravane Again and the Approach of Cease-Fire

Following the recapture of Khong Sedone the two irregular GMs withdrew to MR III and the defense of Khong Sedone was left to the regulars. At this time, rumors of a cease-fire became more pronounced and, on orders from Vientiane, I developed a plan to make one last big effort which could result in the seizure of both Paksong and Saravane, major political objectives in the event of any cease-fire. I would launch an all-out effort to seize these cities and hold them until a cease-fire was negotiated. The plan called for air-landing two irregular GMs near Saravane, and one irregular GM near Lao Ngam on the northwest-southeast axis, halfway between Paksong and Khong Sedone. Two regular GMs would be in reserve along with the newly formed GM 43 which although as yet untested in sustained combat, had acquitted itself very well in actions near Pakse.

This operation was developed and coordinated over a one month period. During this time, the North Vietnamese also were regrouping. The 19th and 39th Infantry Regiments were reconstituted; then in October 1972, the North Vietnamese launched attacks against Khong Sedone and again recaptured the city, their assault infantry swimming the flooded Sedone River at night. This left MR IV faced with a critical decision.

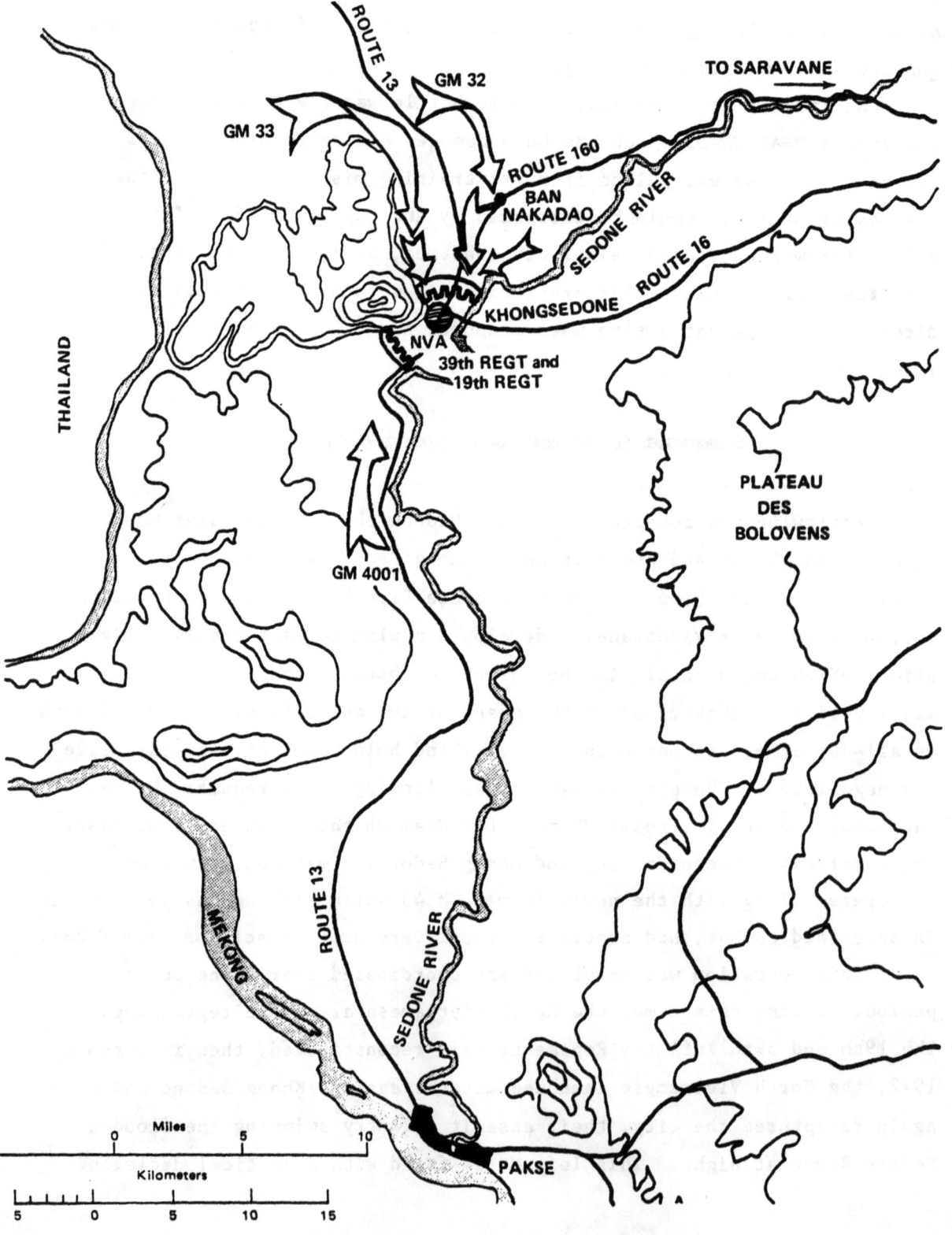

Map 13 — The Battle of Khong Sedone

The planning for the major offensive had been completed and the units involved were in various stages of preparation for the attack on Saravane. I decided that the operation would continue with a regular GM being given the mission of recapturing Khong Sedone. Although this reduced the reserves immediately available to support the operation, the potential gains were worth the risk.

With this decision, GM 42 was air-landed near the Saravane airstrip, unfortunately near the training area for the 39th Infantry Regiment. After considerable difficulty, half of the GM was landed and secured the airstrip. By the time the strip was secure however, all of the USAF helicopters taking part had been hit and were unable to continue. Fortunately, Air America was able to continue the lift until the entire GM was in the landing zone, but with the loss of the helicopters, the airlift of GM 41 was not accomplished on the following day as planned. GM 42 was ordered to move to the northwest of Saravane and locate and secure a landing strip for GM 41. This they did after several days of searching. Finally, GM 41 was inserted and the attack on Saravane began. The delay in the airlift of GM 41 had enabled the North Vietnamese to regroup and the two GMs faced considerable resistance before finally capturing the city. Sinultaneous with this airlift, the GM attacking Khong Sedone was able to push into the city aided by the diversion provided by the Saravane operation.

To further complicate the problems of the NVA at Paksong and Khong Sedone, GM 33 was successfully air-landed into the Lao Ngam area and began search and destroy operations. Shortly after it was inserted, it succeeded in destroying five and damaging another three tanks, putting a severe dent in the armor threat in MR IV. These tanks were destroyed in an ingeniously devised ambush by the GM commander using antitank mines, 3.5-inch rocket launchers and LAW. This victory over the Communist armor represented the single most successful Lao operation against armor in the entire war.

As events later unfolded, it would have been better to have delayed the attacks. Their principal objective was the securing of as much territory as possible before a cease-fire. The attacks were made with the knowledge that the irregulars would not be able to hold the ground for any sustained period. The negotiations dragged on for six months before they were finally signed in February 1973. By the time the cease-fire was signed, all of the population centers captured in these attacks were back in North Vietnamese hands.

Throughout these campaigns, the Pathet Lao posed absolutely no threat in MR IV. Had it been a case of the Neutralists and Rightists against the Pathet Lao, no territory would have been lost to the Communists.

After initial successes in all phases of the operation, the forces involved began to construct defenses in preparation for the coming North Vietnamese counteroffensive. The counteroffensive began to materialize in late November 1972 when the NVA 9th Infantry Regiment was redeployed north from the Paksong area and committed against GMs 41 and 42 at Saravane. Despite this move, the GMs held their ground, although Communist artillery fire was becoming increasingly heavy. In one attack, GM 41 headquarters suffered a direct hit by a 122-mm field gun round which completely demolished the command post, killing all except the GM commander who escaped unscathed.

Fortunately for the irregulars, just when the NVA attacks were becoming more severe, the intensified U.S. bombing of North Vietnam was going on and North Vietnamese morale was noticeably lowered. Also, during this time increasing numbers of USAF strike sorties were being made available to MR IV. These factors served to sustain the irregulars through December 1972 and into January 1973, but by this time the North Vietnamese had massed sufficient force to overrun Saravane and GM 43 was committed to save the situation. Almost as soon as it was committed it uncovered what was to be the largest NVA ammunition cache yet discovered in the war, near where Route 23 crossed the Sedone River to the west of Saravane. Two B-52 strikes were later employed to destroy this ammunition dump when the limited resources of the irregulars were unable to do the job and increasing strong North Vietnamese pressure forced the GM to continue toward Saravane.

Just as the battered GMs 41 and 42 were being gathered for a coordinated attack to recapture Saravane again in early February 1973, GM 43 bumped into the newly committed 101st NVA Regiment south of Saravane. Confusion in air support resulted in the Communist attack dispersing the GM and the attack against Saravane never materialized. The confusion resulted when I, as the MR IV commander, realizing the dire straits of GM 43, called a tactical emergency in order to divert sufficient air, both RLAF and USAF, to save GM 43. Unfortunately, the FAC overhead had an inexperienced backseater and never realized what was going on, while an American, also unfamiliar with the situation, cancelled the tactical emergency and sufficient air support did not result at the critical time. By the time a more experienced FAC could be sent to the area and air support again requested, the GM had been overrun. The failure of the attack against Saravane and the resulting loss of one GM can be directly attributed to the poor communications between an inexperienced FAC and his back-seater, and to an inexperienced individual making the wrong decision at the most critical time. The lesson learned in this exercise was that the MR commander must have absolute control of his forces and their support, otherwise disaster can result.

With this event the battle for Saravane was lost. The only remaining option was to deploy the battered GMs in a delaying action to the west of Saravane in an effort to keep the enemy as far from Khong Sedone as possible. This was done and the GMs were able to hold the Communists 19 kilometers to the east of Khong Sedone at the end of the war.

Although the operations against Khong Sedone, Paksong, Saravane and Lao Ngam had been launched with high hopes, the real objectives of the operations were not realized. In retrospect, a later launch date for the operations may have achieved better results. It is also possible that the NVA were at the same time preparing for a final assault on Pakse and that the friendly forces would have been tied up just defending Pakse and more territory would have been lost by the end of the war. In any event, the operations restored Khong Sedone to RLA control and kept the North Vietnamese away from Pakse itself, a major accomplishment.

In the last two years of heavy fighting in Laos, 1971 and 1972, fierce and costly battles were fought for control of the terrain along the western edge of the panhandle as the NVA sought to secure this extension of its logistical system. Although several key positions changed hands more than once during these months, the NVA control of

the corridor from Saravane to Attopeu was firm as the cease-fire approached. Furthermore, despite great efforts and sacrifices by Laos forces, Paksong, in the heart of the Bolovens Plateau was in enemy hands.

CHAPTER V

Developments Following the February 1973 Cease-Fire

Agreement to Restore Peace and Achieve National Concord

After long and difficult discussions between the RLG and the Pathet Lao representatives, an agreement to end the war was reached on February 21, 1973, and after agreement on protocols it was officially signed on September 14, 1973 in Vientiane. *(Appendix A and B)* This brought about a state of jubilation among the Laotians and their neighboring countries who shared their feelings because they all thought it meant the country would now be able to live in peace.

As far as the ruling government was concerned, it meant long hours of hard work. First, a coalition was formed in Vientiane with hopes that a system of government based on the principles of democracy would evolve. A new joint national political council was assembled in the capital of Luang Prabang to write a new constitution with new laws and regulations to replace the existing constitution which had been written in the early colonial days. Like the council of government that had formed in Vientiane, the coalition was comprised of 16 members from each side of the elected government, and 10 members from the "non-political" group. These latter representatives were to be nationalists without previous records of participation with the Communists. The political council's main mission was to solve the economic and other problems that faced the country, taking the place of the old national assembly.

After the Vientiane agreement and protocols were signed, there was a great urge to bring about a state of unity between the two cities of

Vientiane and Luang Prabang and to work together to build a neutral country. A joint police force was formed, chosen in equal numbers from the two sides. Another joint force was formed to provide protection for members of the coalition government and the political council. As the Pathet Lao had no police force of its own, its military force was allowed to be its component of the police force.

One of the main concerns after the cease-fire was that the fighting still continued. Orders had been issued from the high commands of both sides that all fighting was over and units were to remain in position until further notice. A mixed commission was put into operation to help avoid confrontations. It was very interesting and, needless to say, a surprise to us to learn from the Pathet Lao that they had never had the NVA on their side. In any case, after the cease-fire the fighting that continued was caused by the NVA units still in Laos; many North Vietnamese prisoners were caught during this period of time. Finally, an agreement was negotiated that made us hopeful that all the foreign troops would be withdrawn from Laos immediately.

The signing of the Agreement for the Restoration of Peace and Reconciliation in Laos on 21 February 1973 made the right-wing Lao political group and the Army's high ranking officers supporting the rightist ideology angry with the prime minister, Prince Souvannaphouma, who had put severe pressure on the government delegations, political and military, to force acceptance of the Pathet Lao final proposal. The Rightists had the same feeling toward some U. S. Embassy authorities who had pressured them by saying that no support or aid of any kind would be provided by the U. S. to the RLG if the Pathet Lao proposal was not accepted. For the rightwing group, the signing of that document constituted an act of surrender to the Pathet Lao. The Rightists had fought for many years to free the country from occupation by NVA which had supported the Pathet Lao since the end of World War II. They understood clearly the North Vietnamese goal and could anticipate what would happen next. Furthermore, some of the members of the government, as well as some ranking army officers, were among the leaders of the independence movement in Laos since 1944, some of them even before the surrender of the Imperial Japanese Forces. They considered themselves the true Lao nationalists and deplored the agreement that would perpetuate North Vietnam's control over Laotian affairs. But Souvannaphouma and the American Ambassador, Charles Whitehouse, told us that the Pathet Lao would respect the cease-fire and insist only on the dissolution of the irregular forces maintained, through American support, by the RLG. But this was not the case. Immediately following the cease-fire, the PL began working toward the complete elimination of both the regular and irregular forces of the RLG.

To the Pathet Lao, with the political agreement in hand, the next step was to implement it without delay. Behind the bamboo curtain, every means to exploit every clause to Pathet Lao advantage was carefully prepared; all political cadres were trained in North Vietnam before being dispatched to our zone. Their troops were mainly recruited from the minorities and they had received their political indoctrination partly in North Vietnam and partly in the Pathet Lao occupied areas while the discussion on the protocols of the agreement was going on in Vientiane. On the government side, we believed that time was working to our advantage, while the other side believed the same. They needed enough time for indoctrination of their troops and to receive materiel from the supporting allies.

The agreement was widely discussed at all levels of society, from the morning market fish sellers, the tricycle drivers, up to the high ranking civil servants, each of them drawing their own conclusions as to how the situation would or should be resolved. Many who had relatives on the Pathet Lao side were trying to get in touch with them because if the Pathet Lao became stronger and took control of the country, they might be supported by these relatives. Another group of civil servants, who were not satisfied with the government, hoped to see the Communists come into power so that they could obtain more important posts or higher positions. There were many like that; those who were fired because of corruption or misbehavior, or for lack of capability.

Many political and military leaders in the rightwing group had believed that the prime minister, politically the head of the Neutralists, would be their leader, particularly since Prince Boun Oum and General Phoumi Nosavan had released their hold of the rightwing command. The leader next in line was Mr. Leuam Insixiengmay, a permanent member of the government, but he had proved himself too weak to face the mounting struggle with the Pathet Lao so, after discussions, the rightwing leaders agreed to let Souvannaphouma head them politically.

This rightwing support gave him the power he needed to execute his unity and neutralism policy. He first exercised this power by filling the joint national political council of 42 members; 16 from the government side, 16 from the Pathet Lao, and 10 from the country's qualified elements appointed by both sides. Of course, the 16 members to be chosen from the government side had to be very strong supporters of his neutralism. Unfortuantely, those selected either had negative viewpoints or were old and out of all political activities with no sense of national policy.

Adding to the problem for the rightwing, among the 10 members to be chosen from "qualified people" were trouble makers who had initiated demonstrations against the constitutional institutions, the national assembly, those who proclaimed Souvannaphouma as the father of neutralism, and included members of the civil service who for various reasons were not satisfied with their positions and leaned toward the Pathet Lao movement. In the same council, the appointment of the vice president along with his nephew gave a clear picture of the political game the prince was playing. Souvannaphouma was a very experienced and wise politician, and he knew how to manage the game. Even before and right after the agreement was signed, his personal staff spread the word that in the forthcoming coalition government, the prince was looking for a younger generation; young men to devote and associate themselves to genuine neutralism and to support him as the one and only father of that policy. This was enough to excite all the young group who called themselves "educated" because they had graduated from French colleges and universities. Among them were those who had acted as representatives of the Communists students' "quartier latin" in Paris. They had shown their support for the Pathet Lao even while occupying top positions in the government. So a kind of political party of the "educated elements" was formed by the name of "Movement of the Youth Front" consisting of a president who was director of the *Service Geographic*.[1] He had been associated

---

[1] Mr. Chansamone Varavong

with the beginnings of *Lao Issara*, a nationalist movement during the early years of 1944-1945. His father, Mr. Khun One Varavong, was a retired civil servant who had held the position of governor of a southern province and he was not on good terms with Prince Boun Oum, ruler of the area and chief of the rightwing group.

The movement started off smoothly and staff members kept contact with all political parties and influential members, asking for guidance and moral support. Later, one of the members, Dr. Somphou Oudomvilay, was chosen to be in the coalition cabinet as secretaire d'etat (deputy state secretary) for economics under a Pathet Lao minister (secretary).[2] Their ambition was not to stop there. As graduate students from colleges and universities, they believed that it was time for them to have a greater share in the government. Their disruptive activities pleased the Pathet Lao whose goal was to interfere and disorganize the existing administration. Supported by some unsatisfied civil servants in the ministry of post, telegraph and telecommunication, the director for administration publicly denounced his director-general, Mr. Khamleuang Sayarath, for not treating his subordinates well and for incompetency. Being himself a member of the Youth Front, the director-general tried to call on the Front for support, but to no avail because the director of administration, Mr. Satasinh was supported by the pro-Pathet Lao elements in different departments. It was a successful test of power; with Pathet Lao support even a movement against a Youth Front member could succeed. Furthermore, they demonstrated to Souvannaphouma that the Youth Front totally supported his policy and in

---

[2] Dr. Somphou Oudomvilay was a well-educated man, having been schooled in France, and he was ambitious. Like so many of the young, educated elite, he was easily convinced that the Pathet Lao wished a true coalition government with shared power and responsibilities and he was eager to become an influential member of the new elite. But like nearly all other non-Communists who sought security and position among the Pathet Lao, his enjoyment of prominence in the government was brief. The Pathet Lao kept him only for as long as they wished to exploit his status as a non-Communist. Eighteen months after assuming office, Dr. Somphou Oudomvilay, removed from office and perceiving that his future was indeed bleak if his very life was not threatened, gathered his family together and silently escaped across the Mekong to safety and freedom in Thailand. He now lives quietly in France.

his view, placed them in an advantageous position for appointments to the joint national political council or other political posts where the prince had full power for selection and appointments.

To all these internal troubles, another even more active and powerful threat came into existence: the Student Federation, a strongly left-inclined organization which openly received economic support from the Pathet Lao and from Communist embassies in Vientiane. While the young "educated group" centered its efforts in the capital city, the Student Federation, besides being very active in Vientiane, had branch organizations in all the important provinces such as Luang Prabang, Thakhek, Savannakhet, and Pakse. The ruling committee members travelled about the country to extend their activities and organize the population in areas where some complaints against the administration had been registered. They used demonstrations to oust some of the city and provincial authorities.

Souvannaphouma had a constitutional problem with regard to the peace agreement. Under the Laos' constitution, any agreement with a foreign country or between the Lao of different groups must be submitted to the national assembly for approval. The prince could not see any possibility that the agreement would be approved by that institution, although the national assembly had asked the government to send the agreement to it for debate. Having no constitutional way to close or abolish the national assembly, Souvannaphouma used the Student Federation, supported by the Pathet Lao civilians and other pro-left movements to demand the permanent closing of the assembly. This tactic succeeded because the mixed police force was powerless to interfere and support the assembly and all army units were restricted to their respective camps. When demonstrations against a government agency occurred, the police were called but took no action. The lack of governmental power and the lack of any rightwing activities discouraged conscientious government civil servants for they knew their own careers could be easily ruined with no protection from any quarter.

What was Souvannaphouma's purpose in creating or permitting all the unrest during his administration? He thought that the rightwing was too powerful politically and militarily, and that the agreement would be difficult or impossible to implement if a balance of force could not be achieved. The rightwing was not totally prepared for these rampant attacks and belatedly realized that it could not depend on government protection for their political activities.

Right after the protocol was signed on 14 September 1973, the first contingent of Pathet Lao troops started to land in Luang Prabang and Vientiane. They were followed by uncounted support material of all kinds, from anti-aircraft weapons down to daily food[3]. The quantities and types of materiel were exempt from inspection. Prince Souphanouvong, the leader of the Pathet Lao and Souvannaphouma's half brother, had a tacit agreement to this effect with Souvannaphouma. So every time a Pathet Lao unit arrived and the government delegation wanted to check in accordance with the agreement, the Prime Minister always said, "Let's show them that we have a 'big heart'; it doesn't help us to try to control their shipments; on the contrary, it makes them feel that we don't trust them."

Arriving in Vientiane or in Luang Prabang, small groups of well-trained Pathet Lao propagandists started visiting the villages near their camps, going from house-to-house attacking the "US Imperialists," so-called *reactionnaires* and the Sananikone family, while inside of the camps (they had two in Vientiane) a small dispensary was set up to treat sick people or to distribute some routine medicines. This method was used to call the people together for propaganda and indoctrination. They would talk to them about all the bad things the government was doing to them and keep them for hours before distributing the pills. They emphasized that the people would receive better medical treatment when the Pathet Lao came into control of the country. According to the agreement, the Pathet Lao were to share all administrative activities in Vientiane and Luang Prabrang; for example, traffic, police, customs, airport regulations. Additionally, each ministry had a Pathet Lao minister or *secretaire d'etat*.

---

[3] Russian planes were used to bring the Pathet Lao to the Vientiane airport, while Chinese planes were used to Luang Prabang.

Pathet Lao at Wattay Airport Waiting
to Unload Another Soviet Transport

Soviet Transports Used to Bring the Pathet Lao
into Vientiane at Wattay Airport

In the provincial capitals, where the Pathet Lao military and political cadres were not present, the Student Federation conducted the propaganda activities. They attacked all provincial areas and influential families, criticized the local administration and favoritism, and encouraged the people to demonstrate, calling for replacement of officials by pro-left elements.

In the midst of this unrest, when asked to act to preserve the government, Souvannaphouma always replied:

> "There was misconduct among the civilian servants in the administration at the national and local level. I told them again and again to change, to improve themselves, to be responsible to the population; if they don't recognize their mistakes and change their ways to serve the country, one day someone will tell them to do so and it will be too late."

Violations of the Cease-Fire

After the signing of the Vientiane agreement, the main concern of the Pathet Lao was to weaken the Royal Lao Army. The political and propaganda activities of the PL became so widespread throughout the country that the officers of the RLA became alarmed and they felt a military *coup* was imminent. After the PL deployed troops into Vientiane and Luang Prabang, and as the rumors flew that a military *coup* was possible, and further concerned about the presence of the NVA units still in their country, many Rightist leaders, and Prime Minister Souvannaphouma as well, believed that the most important goal was to rid the country of the NVA. Because he trusted his younger half brother, Prince Souphanouvong, the leader of the PL, and considered him to be an honorable member of their royal family, he had no great fear of the PL. But they had both failed to realize that the NVA would take over their country and replace the regime by a People's Republic just as the Communists had done in other parts of the world where they had gained control.

Right after the signing of the cease-fire agreement, all American military personnel and regular and irregular logistical support personnel left Laos. However, the PL, who had constantly declared that their main concern was to get the foreign troops out of Laos, did not want to discuss the remaining NVA units. They protested that their withdrawal was not subject to any international control, referring to the International Commission of Control which was established by the Geneva Accord, 1954. On the other hand, when the RLG asked the U. S. Government for logistics support, press conferences were held to inform the world of the events.

This situation gave us the opportunity to put pressure on the PL. Some diplomats, favorable to our cause, agreed with the directions we were taking and also advised the NVA to leave the country. Many high ranking officers of the army, as members of the military subcommittee of the Vientiane agreement, met with the prime minister several times asking him to demand the departure of the NVA.

As the discussions on the agreement continued, it was reported that in every PL unit there were NVA soldiers disguised in PL uniforms; others who spoke Laotian left the units to stay among the civilian population, while the NVA main forces had withdrawn from the fighting zones to seek shelter with the PL. As the Pathet Lao continued to bring in their troops, vehicles and food, and all other uncounted and uninspected items, some North Vietnamese military and political cadres were slipping in. The PL also brought in heavy weapons which violated the agreement.

Not only were there violations in Vientiane in which the prime minister showed his favoritism for the PL, but clashes often occurred in the field between the two forces and the results were similar. If the outcome of the fighting was in favor of the PL, our request for an investigation by the government was always delayed or ignored by the prime minister saying, "I will talk about it to Prince Souphanouvong." If, on the other hand, our troops occupied PL ground, commanders at all levels of the army were requested to give an explanation.

As far as the panhandle was concerned, only minor skirmishes marred the cease-fire. In MR IV, we successfully repelled all Pathet Lao attempts to expand its territorial holdings. Meanwhile, the NVA continued its improvements and massive movements along the roads through the panhandle to South Vietnam. For our part, we remained in our garrisons and manned our outposts while our new government in Vientiane began dismantling our army.

Exploiting the political favoritism they enjoyed from the prime minister, the PL, after occupying the strategic position at Sala Phoukhoun at Routes 7 and 13 between Luang Prabang and Vientiane, were in position to move troops farther south to threaten the government's defenses along the main road leading to the country's capital. There was heavy fighting in this region, but as we could not reinforce our positions because of the prohibition banning all troop movement, we lost critical areas. During the larger scale attacks, our American logistics support counterparts told us that air and artillery ammunition supplies would be provided only if we continued to fight against the PL. The Americans told us this, but our chief of government did not tell us to stand and fight. He wanted to know "if we attacked the PL or were we being attacked by them. Did we have the legal right for defense?" In other words, were the RLA forces really adequately provoked into military action by a PL encroachment or attack?

It was clearly understood by the military that Prime Minister Souvannaphouma had helped bring about our weakened military and political situation by his refusal to take a stand against the Communists at times when it was so necessary.

Reduction of Royal Lao Military Strength

Among the first proposals made by the Pathet Lao at the coalition meeting was to call for a reduction of the military budget. Their reasoning was that Laos was entering into a new political phase of "national concord and reconciliation" and its meager funds should be invested in the reconstruction of the country and not in defense. Their efforts to weaken the RLA were made through the ministries of defense and finance. On the government's side, the ministry of defense had held meetings that kept the army authorities at all levels informed of just what terms were being implemented. Finally notice was sent out that reductions would be forthcoming on a gradual basis. With the approval of the U. S. authorities who were supporting our army, the defense ministry set up a plan to reduce the existing 55,000-man Regular Army and the 38,000-man Irregular Forces to a combined level of 48,000 or 45,000, to be accomplished in a period of three years. The progress being made in this reduction of the Regular Army was discussed at every staff meeting attended by responsible authorities from all military regions. After numerous meetings the demobilization plans were finally drawn up.

During the planning process it had not been easy for those who recognized what our people had endured during the long war, remembering the fine performance of our troops who had fought with such determination and courage. Furthermore, our problems were made even more difficult by the fact that the PL had begun to use psychological warfare against our soldiers. The Laotians have a proverb that says, "killing the buffaloes after the harvest and the soldiers after the war is bad policy." This proverb offered us some comprehension as to just how difficult our situation actually was during this period of time.

The word "demobilization" was practically never used in this operation for fear it would demoralize our soldiers. But training for and the transfer of people to civilian administration was often mentioned. Special instructions were given to the ministries of education, interior, health, and public works to accept within their respective administrations soldiers released from the army. Positions were offered to all officers wishing to make transfers to these ministries. In the army, the reduction was received by many of the young, intelligent, and well-trained officers as a blessing in disguise. They felt they had more opportunities offered to them in civilian jobs than for promotions in the military service. The senior officers, who had not been afforded the same advantages that were offered to the young officers, felt a sense of insecurity. To hasten the reduction process, the defense ministry encouraged senior army officers to take their retirement early, but promised them it would be on full retirement pension.

If the implementation of the resettlement program presented many problems in the Regular Army, it provoked even more problems for the irregulars. The irregular officers had been detached from the Regular Army to assume civilian positions in the villages such as teaching school and handling administrative positions. Some were the unwanted elements expelled from the Regular Army and some were foreign mercenaries from the neighboring countries. However, in order to accomplish the program, units of irregulars had to be transferred into the regulars, using the same TOE. To do this, army regulations had to be strictly followed concerning age and nationality. Therefore, the foreign mercenaries were the first to be removed from their units. The second step was to dismiss the "unwanted elements" who had formerly served in the Regular Army but had not qualified for differing reasons. The third step was to dismiss the senior local village chiefs and some of the others who had been released from the army to serve in their villages. There finally remained the duties of the region commanders, under whom all these units had been serving, to submit to the RLA the reorganization plans of their battalions, abiding by the rules and regulations of the RLA TOE.

The Defense Ministry encountered an enormous number of problems in the reduction program of the RLA. Problems arose not only from within the army itself, but also from pressures that came from the Pathet Lao. All through the countryside the PL had spread propaganda against the injustice and ingratitude of the army for dismissing the soldiers after having so badly "used" them. The result of this propaganda was that many of the RLA soldiers started to support the Pathet Lao openly. It was also a major reason for the success of the Pathet Lao propaganda in bringing about a state of unrest among the people.

Finally, after more than one year of implementation the demobilization program was still not completely accomplished, although at least 50 to 60 percent of the troops left the army during this difficult period. GMs were reduced to battalions and the irregular units were integrated into the regular force. The RLA no longer presented any threat to the Ho Chi Minh trail in the panhandle, or anywhere else in Laos, for that matter. The DRV found it possible to deploy major units from Laos to North and South Vietnam. Among the most significant redeployments was the 968th NVA Division from the panhandle to the central highlands of South Vietnam where it participated in the spring offensive of 1975.

When South Vietnam capitulated on 30 April 1975, we in Laos knew that our time was running out. As many as eight thousand more Pathet Lao troops in civilian clothes, intermingled with disguised NVA soldiers, began infiltrating Vientiane. After a high ranking Rightist official was assassinated, the minister of defense elected to escape into Thailand. This meant that the deputy minister, Kham Oune Boupha, a Pathet Lao, became the senior defense official. The Communist takeover was accelerating rapidly.

Kham Ouane Boupha insisted that a complete integration of Pathet Lao and RLA units proceed immediately in Military Regions III and IV. I was still in command in MR IV and I knew that Neutralists and Rightists could not survive with Pathet Lao officers in our units. Nevertheless, Souvannaphouma agreed with the Pathet Lao defense minister, and Pathet Lao battalions began moving into our zones of control, past our outposts and the stakes that had been driven into the ground by mutual agreement and marked the zones under the control of the two sides.

On 18 May, not even three weeks after the fall of South Vietnam, the Pathet Lao battalions marched into the city of Pakse, the site of my region headquarters. At eight o'clock in the morning, battalion after battalion in full battle dress paraded through the streets of my province capital, flanked on each side by rows of civilians, old men, women with babies and children. The Communist troops entered my garrisons and camped alongside my outnumbered, outgunned troops.

Three days later I received orders from Vientiane to report to Chinaimo Army Camp in the capital to attend a seminar on the new government and defense policies. All region commanders, subdivision commanders and regimental commanders were there, as was each region's chief of staff. I was very uneasy during the two-week session in Vientiane as I was being subjected to the strong dose of anti-American, pro-Communist propaganda, but my greatest concern was what was happening to my command at Pakse while I was detained in Vientiane. One of my worst expectations was realized when word reached me that two of my colonels, who happened to be in Souvannaphouma's Neutralist faction, had been arrested by the Pathet Lao.

I immediately went to see Souvannaphouma to protest this illegal act in my command. I pointed out to the prime minister that we could not work out our differences with the Pathet Lao if they ignored the law and exercised raw power to assume control in regions that were under the authority of duly appointed officers of the RLG. I made it clear that the two colonels were members of his political faction and that he should act immediately to secure their release. I asked him for an order which I would present to the minister of defense that would require him to have my colonels set free.

Souvannaphouma agreed and, with me standing by his desk, took his pen and personally wrote the order. I took the paper and presented it to Kham Ouane Boupha. He read it, smiled, and said that this matter was of no concern to the prime minister; that it was only an affair to be settled in the military region. In other words, the minister of defense ignored the lawful order of his own prime minister. A cold wave of fear and despair passed over me. It was obvious now that Souvannaphouma could no longer govern. He could not even moderate the excesses the Pathet Lao would bring upon us.

During the second week of the seminar, Kham Ouane Boupha told us that the new armed forces of Laos would be organized with Pathet Lao soldiers integrated at every echelon, from squad to the general staff, and there would be Pathet Lao commanders at each echelon. Furthermore, all RLA officers, noncommissioned officers and soldiers would report to their units and begin working in the fields, planting and harvesting their own rice, manioc and vegetables to support their units, since there would be no government funds for this purpose.

Our concern for our families and our future became severe, and our morale sank to the depths of despair. I left Vientiane without even paying my final respects to the prime minister and returned to my headquarters at Pakse. There I gathered my family and the few things we could carry with us, returned to Vientiane and escaped across the broad Mekong to Nong Khai, Thailand. My long career as a soldier in the service of my country was over because my army had been reduced to a fragment, then devoured by the Communists in the name of reconciliation and concord.

CHAPTER VI

Observations and Conclusions

Successes and Failures

Although the reduced American commitment and the NVA's determined, reinforced offensive throughout Indochina combined to ultimately defeat Laos, there occurred some major successes during the intensified war period, May 1971 to February 1973, in MR IV. In the midst of the North Vietnamese offensive, we managed a complete reorganization of the regular and irregular forces in the region, creating new organizations and units more suited to meeting the major Communist combat formations. To control these new factors, we completely reorganized the military region staff, constituting a TOC with adequate facilities to fight the major battles in the region. Despite the fact that the irregular GMs could not hold territory in the face of superior NVA firepower and manpower, even Ambassador Whitehouse acknowledged that the defensive operations of the GM 41 near Saravane at the end of the war were unparalleled. This GM absorbed over 60 percent casualties and still remained a viable combat force in the field. GM 42 also sustained extremely high casualties and was still in the field at the end of the war although admittedly less combat effective than GM 41.

Another major success was the defense of the territory in the hands of the RLA at the end of May 1971. Despite Communist efforts in MR IV, they were unable to gain and hold any appreciable territory following their victory at Paksong in May 1971. Compared with past performances of the regular and irregular forces in MR IV, this had to be considered a major accomplishment. Credit also must go to the MR III GMs, particularly GMs 32 and 33 for their efforts in MR IV.

Increased air support from the USAF during December 1972 and into January and February 1973 also played a major role in the defense of MR IV. Without this air support, the defense of such a wide area in MR IV, with the limited forces available, would not have been possible. Employment of air power, and the training of small unit commanders in its use, were major accomplishments. Another aspect of the successful upgrading of air support in MR IV was the increased combat proficiency of the RLAF. The small RLAF unit at Pakse improved remarkably during the period of intensified war. By the war's end they were the most proficient in all of Laos and were readily responsive to the needs of the ground forces. A major factor in this improvement was the training and employment of the Lao FACs which improved communications with the supported ground unit considerably.

Finally, the streamlined command and control structure instituted at MR IV headquarters to the GM commanders and the subordinate battalion commanders was responsible in some measure for the tactical successes we enjoyed. A similar structure was also developed for managing the civilian duties of the military region commander. This structure eliminated much of the internal fighting between battalion commanders, although the patronage system for certain battalions still existed at the end of the war, particularly the battalions controlled by Phasouk and family. It is unfortunate but true that the MR IV staff and troop compliment were just attaining a state of proficiency to fight the war when it ended. Unfortunately political considerations required that the major strike elements of the combat forces in MR IV were rendered practically combat ineffective by the end of the war, but this was due to prolonged commitment in the field which would not have been necessary had the future of a long war presented itself. The system for rotating units from front line operations to the rear for retraining and refitting was just beginning to pay dividends when the last major operation of the war was launched and the system was abandoned in favor of attempting to retain territory for political reasons. It is reasonable to say that the continuing conflict in MR IV must have been a surprise to the North Vietnamese and this forced them to commit more forces than they had initially planned, just to hold what they had. This probably reduced the troops available for employment in South Vietnam.

Probably the most significant failure was the inability to end the continuing conflict with the Phasouk family which detracted from the war effort and caused some dissention in the officer ranks within MR IV. This problem continued from the time Phasouk was assigned as Chief of Staff of the Armed Forces in Vientiane to the end of the war. It is very difficult to fight a war while looking over your shoulder to make sure you are not being set up by the friendly forces.

Another problem never resolved was the lack of positive unified control of the military forces in MR IV. Each operation had to be separately negotiated with Phasouk's factions and then with GM commanders. Never was control firmly established. The very nature of irregular forces makes them extremely difficult to control but while the Lao irregulars were most responsive militarily to the MR commander, other factions remained beyond his control until the end of the war. The regular forces were little better initially. Although this problem was largely remedied by the end of the war, it proved a serious distraction at critical times, particularly during the fight for Khong Sedone when it was necessary to relieve the BV 44 commander (a Phasouk assignment) for serious breaches of military discipline. The repercussions of this relief dragged on for over six months and continued to be a distracting factor even later.

The failure of the support system to provide timely logistic and administrative support to committed troops was another serious shortcoming. Although significant improvements were made during the year just prior to the end of the war, this problem continuously haunted military commanders at all levels. Equipment vitally needed in MR IV remained in Vientiane or was only partially shipped to Pakse. As an example, bulldozers were vital to maintaining lines of communications in MR IV during the period of rapidly changing situations. These bulldozers either remained in Vientiane or spare parts were not available. There was little that could be accomplished at the military region level to improve this intolerable situation.

Administrative problems remained to the end of the war. Medical facilities were totally inadequate for handling the increased casualties caused by the intensified fighting. The hospital in Pakse was constantly overcrowded and medicine was in short supply. This adversely affected morale at a time when the highest possible morale was needed. This fact also contributed to the continuing replacement/recruitement problems which plagued regular as well as irregular units to the end of the war. It was seldom possible to get more than 300 men in the field in the regular battalions although their assigned strength was, in some cases, over 800 men. Although some of the problem must be attibuted to failure on the part of the commanders, much of it was due to the fact that a battalion commander had to carry his sick and wounded on the rolls until they could be either returned to duty or processed out of the army, an extremely difficult procedure. As a result, a battalion might have had up to 150 men who were physically unable to perform combat duty, but replacements could not be recruited due to a manpower ceiling.

Command problems have been previously discussed but one particular one deserves emphasis: this was the refusal to recognize that irregular units could not stay together beyond 90 to 120 days in the field. The optimum time to pull them out was when they were approaching 90 days in combat. At this time they still had unit integrity and desertion had not become a problem. Much beyond this time they began to fall apart. When the disintegration began, it culminated rapidly in total combat ineffectiveness. In many instances, this reality was recognized but could not be remedied due to the tactical situation. In these instances, the unit was just left in the field until it lost all combat effectiveness and then was completely rebuilt. After about a year's experience with these problems, a rotation system was instituted but soon abandoned when the push for territory began as talks on ending the war progressed. Had this system been maintained, it is quite likely that at least two irregular GMs would have been combat ready at war's end, although some territory may have been lost.

The continuing rumors of integrating the irregulars into the RLA, and the procedures which were implemented to fulfill this objective toward the end of the war, had serious adverse effects on irregular morale, particularly on the officers, because these men faced a loss of pay as well as prestige on integration; they could not be integrated at the grades they held in the irregulars and, in some cases, could not be integrated at all. Following the cease-fire, this became a major problem which continued up through the time when the Communists assumed control of Laos.

Observations

Militarily and politically also, Laos was considered the "well moderated people" of the Indochinese Union. From 1893 until 1945, only three uprisings took place, all of them staged not by plains-dwelling Lao, but by the mountaineers, particularly the warlike tribes living near the Chinese border. In 1934 in southern Laos, a very serious rebellion took place among the Alcak and Lavea tribes of the Bolovens Plateau which, initially caused by intertribal warfare involving kidnapping and human sacrifices, developed into a bloody, no-quarters-given jungle war. The French succeeded in restoring order in the Bolovens after almost two years of fighting but the primitive tribes of the area never really reconciled themselves to outside control. This accounted for the difficulty the RLG encountered in trying to counter the invasion of this part of Laos by NVA. The tribes displayed little loyalty to the government and, although they did not willingly support the NVA either, their independence and indifference to the struggle made it relatively easy for the North Vietnamese to impose enough control over the corridor they required in southern Laos to secure the flow of men and materiel into South Vietnam and Cambodia. Of course, although it is unlikely that the Communist government of Laos will be able to secure the active loyalty or support of the panhandle mountaineers, or even be able to control local banditry or incidents of insurrection in southern Laos, such lack of control will not be a serious threat to the security of the government in Vientiane and after all, security in this wild, primitive region on the frontier of South Vietnam is no longer vital to North Vietnam's conquest of South Vietnam.

Occupation of and passage through the panhandle of Laos was vital to the NVA in its prosecution of the war in South Vietnam and its support of the Communist rebels in Cambodia. The US Government was aware of this fact, but for reasons beyond the scope of my personal knowledge, chose to be bound, at least overtly, by the provisions of the 1962 Geneva Accords which prohibited the introduction of "foreign" forces into Laos. The DRV ignored this prohibition, and the RLA was too small and too lightly supported to seriously challenge the NVA in southern Laos. Recognizing the reality of this situation, the RLG official position was neutrality, preferring to look upon the contest for control along the Ho Chi Minh trail as a dispute between the opposing sides in the war in Vietnam. But this position could not survive the NVA expansion of its road, trail and river network westward to the Bolovens Plateau. Laos had to fight the NVA for possession of the narrow strip of rich, populated territory along the southern Mekong river.

Still, for reasons not clear to me, US policy persisted in keeping the RLA high command out of the circle of consultation, coordination and cooperation in the prosecution of the war against the common enemy. The most glaring example of this was the US-supported South Vietnamese invasion of Laos along Route 9 to Tchepone in early 1971. Had we been informed, the RLA could have contributed at the least a valuable diversion, at the most a supporting attack, either of which could have enhanced the possibility of success in this campaign.

In February 1971, reacting to South Vietnamese military operations in southern Laos, some 80 percent of the North Vietnamese forces in Laos were deployed in the Royal Government's Military Region III and IV. These forces included infantry battalions, transport, engineer, and communication units; anti-aircraft and artillery units; and advisers to the Pathet Lao.

The NVA was less worried about the RLA than it was about the possibility that American ground troops would move into southern Laos to cut off infiltration and supplies to South Vietnam. Reflections of this anxiety were Radio North Vietnam's frequent broadcasts denouncing alleged plans by the US to establish bases within southern Laos from which to attack North Vietnam. The heavy bombing of the Ho Chi Minh trail by the US Air Force was also bitterly denounced by the North Vietnamese as a violation of the Geneva Accords of 1962. Furthermore, they charged that the US was violating the agreements by introducing ground forces into Laos. Their pronouncements on these subjects fulfilled several functions. On the one hand, by focusing international attention on these issues, they hoped to pressure their enemies into suspending all hostile action in Laos and, perhaps more importantly, to discourage future ground attacks in the trail area. On the other hand, they were signaling that they would respond to such attacks in kind. Whether in response to DRV propaganda or not, the fact is that the US never put any sizeable formation into Laos, and the South Vietnamese Lam Son 719 experience was the only one of its kind.

American and South Vietnamese high ranking officials, even those stationed in Laos, thought that the North Vietnamese flow of troops and materiel moving down to South Vietnam could be effectively interdicted from the air and by small raiding parties. This idea was proven wrong. NVA security was too effective to permit significant interference by our irregulars, and aerial interdiction was hampered by poor visibility. Even though the US had air supremacy, the targets were highly elusive. An effective interdiction campaign requires not only attacks on the supply routes and associated stationary targets such as storage areas, roads and bridges but also the destruction of the vehicles themselves and their cargo.

With American guidance and assistance the RLG responded to the increased NVA threat to southern Laos after the 1970 Cambodian *coup* by reorganizing the irregular forces into larger formations. The concept was that the new battalions and GMs would be able to conduct large raids and spoiling attacks against regular NVA formations, cause high casualties, and withdraw quickly to fight again. The idea was valid, and we constructed a number of highly mobile, aggressive, tough units. Tragically, these hard-hitting units, which lacked the staying power of conventional infantry, were badly misused, partly out of necessity perhaps, but mostly because Vientiane did not understand the concept. The Vientiane leadership was loath to give up any more terrain to the NVA, and our light, efficient, irregular battalions were too often required to try to hold ground against the superior firepower and numbers of regular NVA formations.

The RLG was traditionally deeply concerned almost exclusively with developments in Military Region II because of the threat to the survival of the capital region. The Vientiane people for too long ignored the fact that southern Laos was a strategic area in the Communist plan to gain control of Indochina. Maintaining the seat of government in Vientiane was considered essential, but the developments in south Laos were what really determined the outcome of the war for Cambodia and South Vietnam and, as events proved, for the future of Laos as well.

The central lesson of the entire Laos experience is that however well intentioned and sincere may be the proponents of neutrality for small states, if the geographical position of the state is such that its territory is of vital importance in the military strategy of another more powerful state, that neutrality cannot be maintained. The attempt to maintain neutrality under these conditions in Laos meant that the aggressor, North Vietnam, because of its proximity, its military power and its disregard for even the forms of responsible international behavior, enjoyed a decisive military advantage.

The US, in its attempt to preserve at least the overt appearance of respect for international agreements and for the neutrality of Laos, declined to apply the military force and presence that would have been required to *enforce* Laos neutrality, which in this case could have been done only by physically ejecting the NVA from the Laos panhandle. It is doubly ironic that such enforcement of Laos neutrality would also have secured US and South Vietnamese objectives in Vietnam and Cambodia.

Finally, in the event anyone ever doubted the inseparability of the three major battlefields in Indochina, Laos, South Vietnam and Cambodia, that doubt should by now have been erased. Following two years of relatively little overt activity after the signing of the cease-fire in Laos, the collapse of Cambodia and South Vietnam signaled the abrupt and overwhelming assertion of Pathet Lao power in Laos which completed the destruction of the Neutralist government and its armed forces. North Vietnam's victory was complete. What lies ahead for the remaining non-Communist, free nation of the peninsula is now the question. North Vietnam emerged from the war the most powerful military force in the region. How will it use this power? I believe that the people of mainland Southeast Asia and the world will be treated to their next North Vietnamese lesson in military strategy when the Communists are ready to turn their attention to Thailand.

APPENDIX A

The Agreement on the Restoration
of Peace and Reconciliation in Laos[1]

In response to the august desire of His Majesty the King and the earnest hope of the entire Lao people who wish to end the war soon, to restore and preserve a durable peace, and to achieve national reconciliation to unify the nation, and establish its independence, neutrality, democracy and prosperity so it may play a role in the development of peace in Indochina and Southeast Asia;

Based on the 1962 Geneva Agreement concerning Laos and the current situation in Laos, the Vientiane Government side and the Patriotic Forces side have agreed unanimously as follows:

Chapter I

General Principles

Article 1

(a) The desires of the Lao people to safeguard and exercise their cherished fundamental national rights — the independence, sovereignty, unity and territorial integrity of Laos — are inviolable.

(b) The declaration on the neutrality of Laos of July 9, 1962, and the 1962 Geneva Agreement on Laos are the correct bases for the Kingdom of Laos' foreign policies of peace, independence and neutrality. The parties concerned in Laos, the United States, Thailand and other foreign countries must strictly respect and implement this agreement. The internal affairs of Laos must be conducted by the Lao people only, without external interference.

---

[1] Keesing's Contemporary Archives, April 16-22, 1973, p. 25843.

(c) To achieve the supreme objective of restoring peace, consolidating independence, achieving national concord and restoring national unity, and taking into consideration the present reality in Laos, which has two zones separately controlled by the two sides, the internal problems of Laos must be solved in the spirit of national concord and on the basis of equality and mutual respect, free from pressure or annexation by either side.

(d) To safeguard national independence and sovereignty, achieve national concord and restore national unity, the people's democratic freedoms must be scrupulously observed, which comprise individual freedom, freedom of religion, speech, press, assembly, establishment or political organizations and associations, candidacy and elections, movement and residence, free enterprise, and the right to ownership of private property. All laws, regulations and institutions contrary to these freedoms must be abolished.

Chapter II

Military Provisions

Article 2

Beginning at 12:00 on February 22, 1973, a cease-fire in place will be observed simultaneously throughout the territory of Laos. This includes:

(a) Foreign countries must completely and permanently cease the bombing of the territory of Laos, all acts of intervention and aggression in Laos, and all military involvement in Laos.

(b) All armed forces of foreign countries must completely and permanently cease all military activities in Laos.

(c) The armed forces of the Lao parties must completely cease all military acts that constitute hostilities on the ground and in the air.

Article 3

As soon as the cease-fire goes into effect:

(a) All military acts of assault, annexation, threat or violation on the ground and in the air against the territory temporarily controlled by the other side are strictly prohibited.

(b) All hostile military acts including the activities of bandits and commandos and armed activities and espionage on the ground and in the air are strictly prohibited. In case one side wants to transport food supplies across the territory under the control of the other side, the Joint Commission for Implementation of the Agreement will discuss and lay down a clear-cut procedure for this.

(c) All raids and operations of intimidation, repression and infringement on the lives and property of the people, and all acts of reprisal and discrimination against those who collaborated with the opposite side during the war, shall be strictly prohibited. People who were forced to leave their native villages during the war must be assisted to return there freely to earn their living in accordance with their desires.

(d) The introduction into Laos of military personnel of any type, regular or irregular, and all kinds of weapons and war material of foreign countries, except as provided for the 1954 and 1962 Geneva Agreements, shall be prohibited. In case it is necessary to replace damaged or worn-out weapons and war material, the two sides will discuss this and will make decisions by common agreement.

Article 4

Within 60 days at the latest after the establishment of the Provisional National Union Government and the National Political Consultative Council, the withdrawal of all military personnel and regular and irregular forces from Laos and the dissolution of all military and paramilitary organizations of foreign countries shall be completed. The special forces organized, armed, trained and commanded by foreigners shall be disbanded, and their bases, military positions and strongholds completely dismantled.

Article 5

Each of the two Lao parties shall return to the other party all persons, regardless of nationality, who had been captured or detained because they collaborated with the other party in the war. Their return will be carried out in accordance with the principles agreed upon by the two sides and be completed within 60 days at the latest after the establishment of the Provisional National Union Government and the National Political Consultative Council. Following the completion of the return of captured personnel, each side will have the responsibility to provide the other side with information on those reported missing during the war.

Chapter III

Provisions on Political Affairs

Article 6

Genuinely free and democratic general elections shall be organized to establish the National Assembly and a permanent National Union Government genuinely representing the people of all nationalities in Laos. The procedures and date of the general elections will be discussed and agreed upon by the two sides. Pending the general elections, the two sides shall set up a new Provisional National Union Government and a National Political Consultative Council within 30 days at the latest after the signing of this agreement, to implement the provisions of the agreement and handle State affairs.

Article 7

The new Provisional National Union Government will be composed of representatives of the Vientiane Government and of the Patriotic Forces (Pathet Lao), in equal numbers, and two intellectuals who stand for peace, independence, neutrality and democracy, who will be chosen by common agreement by the two sides. The future Prime Minister will not be included in the two equal numbers of representatives of the two parties.

The Provisional National Union Government will be set up in accordance with special procedures by royal decree of his Majesty the King. It will perform its duties in accordance with principles unamiously agreed upon by both sides. It will have the responsibility to implement the agreement and the political programme agreed upon by the two sides, and especially to implement and maintain the cease-fire, permanently safeguard peace, observe all popular rights and freedoms, practice a foreign policy of peace, independence and neutrality, co-ordinate plans for economic construction and cultural development, and receive and distribute the common aid given by various countries to Laos.

Article 8

The National Political Consultative Council will be an organization of national concord and will be composed of representatives of the Vientiane Government and of the Patriotic Forces in equal numbers, as well as a number of personalities who advocate peace, independence, neutrality and democracy, to be chosen by the two sides by common agreement. It will perform its duties in accordance with the principle of unanimity of the two parties. It has the responsibility to consult with and express views to the Provisional National Union Government on major problems relating to domestic and foreign policies; to support and assist the Provisional National Union Government and the two sides in implementing the agreement in order to achieve national concord; to examine and adopt together the laws and regulations for general election; and to collaborate with the Provisional National Union Government in holding general elections to establish the National Assembly and the permanent National Union Government. The procedures for the establishment of the National Political Consultative Council will be discussed and agreed upon by the two sides, and will be sent to the Provisional National Union Government to be forwarded to His Majesty the King for his decree of appointment. The same procedure will be applied to the dissolution of the National Political Consultative Council.

Article 9

The two sides agree to neutralize the royal capital of Luang Prabang and the city of Vientiane, and to take all measures to guarantee the security and the effective functioning of the Provisional National Union Government and the National Political Consultative Council, and to prevent all acts of sabotage or pressure by any force from within or without.

Article 10

(a) Pending the establishment of the National Assembly and the permanent National Union Government, in the spirit of Article 6 in Chapter II of the joint Zurich communique of June 22, 1961, the two sides will keep the territories under their temporary control, and will endeavor to implement the political programme of the Provisional National Union Government, as agreed upon by both sides.

(b) The two sides will promote the establishment of normal relations between the two zones, and create favorable conditions for the people to move about, make their living, and carry out economic and cultural exchanges with a view to consolidating national concord and bringing about national unification at an early date.

(c) The two parties take note of the declaration of the US Government that it will contribute to healing the wounds of the war and to post-war reconstruction in Indo-China. The Provisional National Union Government will hold discussions with the US Government in connection with such a contribution regarding Laos.

Chapter IV

The Joint Commission for Implementation of the Agreement and the International Commission for Supervision and Control

Article 11

The implementation of this agreement is the responsibility of the two sides concerned in Laos. The two sides will immediately establish a Joint Commission for Implementation of the Agreement, comprising representatives of both sides in equal proportions. This commission will begin functioning immediately after the cease-fire goes into effect. It will perform its tasks in accordance with the principle of discussion and unanimous decision.

Article 12

The International Commission for Control and Supervision established in accordance with the 1962 Geneva Agreement on Laos, composed of representatives of India, Poland and Canada, and with India as chairman, will continue its activities in accordance with the tasks, powers and principles as provided for in the protocol of the said Geneva Agreements.

APPENDIX B

Protocols to the Agreement[1]

Summary of Main Provisions

(1) A Provisional Government of National Union would be formed, headed by a neutral Prime Minister and two Deputy Premiers, one belonging to the Pathet Lao and the other to the Vientiane Government.

(2) Representatives of the Vientiane Government would hold the Defense, Interior, Finance and Education portfolios; Pathet Lao representatives those of Foreign Affairs, Public Works, the Economy and Information; and "persons working for peace, independence, neutrality and democracy" those of Justice and Posts. The Vientiane and Pathet Lao Ministers would each be assisted by a Secretary of State drawn from the other party. A Vientiane Secretary of State would be assigned to one of the neutralist Ministers, and a Pathet Lao Secretary of State to the other.

(3) The Provisional Government would establish a political programme based on the 1962 Geneva Agreements and the recommendations of the National Political Consultative Council, which would preserve the people's liberties, implement a neutral foreign policy, ensure national unity, and "establish a peaceful, independent, neutral, democratic, unified and prosperous Laos."

(4) The Provisional Government would follow the unanimous decisions of the two parties in all important matters.

(5) The National Political Consultative Council would consist of 42 persons, comprising representatives of the two parties and neutralist representatives chosen by the two parties. Between sessions routine business would be managed by a permanent office consisting of five members chosen by each side. The Council would have six committees: a secretariat and commissions for (a) politics, law and general elections, (b) security and defense, (c) foreign affairs and foreign aid, (d) economics and finance, and (e) education and culture.

---

[1] Keesing's Contemporary Archives, November 12-18, 1973, p. 26191.

(6) The Council would permit equally balanced discussion until a consensus was reached. If no consensus was reached the unanimity of the Vientiane Government and the Pathet Lao would be decisive. The Council would meet every six months for a session not exceeding one month, and if necessary the permanent office might call a special session.

(7) The Council would revise the law of 1957 on democratic liberties to adapt it to "current political realities", and would organize democratic general elections.

(8) The officials in the cities of Vientiane and Luang Prabang, which would be neutralized, would be chosen by agreement between the two parties. A joint police force would be set up in the two cities, consisting of 1,000 men from each side in Vientiane and 500 in Luang Prabang, and a battalion of troops from each side would be stationed in each city. Other armed forces would be forbidden to enter them, and military aircraft would be forbidden to fly over these cities.

(9) Provisional cease-fire lines would be established where the two sides' forces were in contact, and troop movements over these lines by land or air were prohibited. The armed forces and police were forbidden to take reprisals against persons who had collaborated with the other side.

(10) Troops and military personnel of foreign countries must be withdrawn within 60 days from the formation of the Provisional Government and the National Political Consultative Council. This provision applied to "military personnel camouflaged in embassies and consulates", except those whose names appeared on the personnel list of diplomatic missions recognized by the Provisional Government.

(11) Troops of both parties were forbidden to accept military equipment from foreign countries. Where replacements were necessary a unanimous decision by both parties was required. Foreign countries were forbidden to use Laotian territory to interfere in the internal affairs of other countries.

(12) "Special forces" organized and armed by other countries must be removed and their bases dismantled.

(13) Each party must release all soldiers taken prisoner and civilian arrested during the hostilities within 60 days from the formation of the Provisional Government.

(14) Refugees had the right to return to their villages.

(15) The two parties would form a Mixed Central Commission consisting of seven representatives of each side to implement the agreement. The International Control Commission would continue its work in collaboration with the Mixed Commission.

Glossary

ADC	Auto Defense de Choc (Self Defense Force)
ADO	Auto Defense Ordinaire (Local Self Defense Force)
ARVN	Army of the Republic of Vietnam (South)
BC	Bataillon Commando
BCL	Bataillon de Chasseurs Laotiens (Infantry Battalion)
BI	Bataillon d'Infanterie
BLL	Bataillon Leger Laos (Light Infantry)
BP	Bataillon Parachutiste
BV	Bataillon Volontaire
DRV	Democratic Republic of Vietnam (North)
FAC	Forward Air Controller
FAN	Forces Armees Neutralistes
FAR	Forces Armees Royales
GB	Guerrilla Battalion
GM	Groupement Mobile
ICC	International Control Commission
JOC	Joint Operations Center
LAW	Light Antitank Weapon
LPLA	Lao People's Liberation Army
MMF/GRL	Mission Militaire Francaise pres le Gouvernement Royal Lao
NLHS	Neo Lao Hak Sat (Lao Patriotic Front)
NVA	North Vietnamese Army
PEO	Program Evaluation Office
PL	Pathet Lao

PLP	People's Laotian Party
PL	People's Party of Laos (Phak Pasason Lao)
P.S.	Pakse site
RLAF	Royal Lao Air Force
RLA	Royal Lao Army
RLG	Royal Lao Government
RO	Requirements Office
SGU	Special Guerrilla Unit
SGU-BN	Special Guerrilla Unit-Battalion
SVN	South Vietnam
TOC	Tactical Operations Center
TOE	Table of Organization and Equipment